Canal of Colombia

The best route in America for a canal between the Atlantic and Pacific Oceans.

Jaime Gómez González, MD

Juan Andrés Moreno, Esq.

Claudia G. Baldwin, Ed. S

Copyrights @ 2020

Proposed New Shield of the Republic of Colombia. LH Flórez

Authors:

Jaime Gómez González, MD

USA Representative CANATCOL, AP

Canatcol66@gmail.com

Juan Andrés Moreno, Esq.

Attorney, Executive Secretary, CANATCOL, AP., Colombia

Claudia G. Baldwin, M. Ed, Ed.S.

President, Sowing Seeds for the Future, USA

www.CANATCOL.com

Dedication

Dedicated to Santa María del Darién, to intercede for the Children of Chocó who die due to hunger and malnutrition.

Disclaimer

This book reflects the views of the authors only, as well as the review of the data obtained from their research and does not reflect the views or policies of CANATCOL, AP.

Neither CANATCOL, AP. nor the authors, make any warranty, express or implied, or assumes any legal liability or responsibility for the accuracy or completeness of any information contained in this book, or process described herein, and assumes no responsibility for anyone's use of the information. Research studies must be done again to confirm the dimensions.

CANATCOL, AP is not responsible for errors or omissions in this report and makes no representations as to the accuracy or completeness of the information.

CANATCOL, AP does not endorse products or companies. Reference in this report to any specific commercial products, process, or service by trade name, trademark, manufacturer, or otherwise, does not constitute or imply its endorsement, recommendation, or favoring by CANATCOL, AP and shall not be used for advertising or service endorsement purposes. Trade or company names appear in this book only because they are essential to the goals of the book.

References and hyperlinks to external web sites do not constitute endorsement by CANATCOL, AP to the linked web sites, or the information, products or services contained therein.

CANATCOL, AP does not exercise any editorial control over the information you may find at these locations.

The authors of the book, wrote this book due to their sincere love for their country, Colombia. They dedicated their time and resources to research the information and contacts and even though they are professionals in the areas of health and law, they do not claim to have expertise in the field of Engineering, Marine Sciences or Canal Construction. They are concerned with the lack of capital resources and services, and the neglect in which the children live in Chocó and their purpose is to advocate for them.

INTEROCEANIC CANAL OF COLOMBIA

Content

- Law 53 of 1984 order to build the Interoceanic Canal of Colombia

8. 21st century:

- Petition to the President of Colombia

- CANATCOL, AP

- Colombian Canal: Interior Navigation

- Excavation of the Canal

- Environmental Studies

9. Bill 2019

10. Business plan

11. Statement of reasons

12. Conclusions

13. Bibliography

14. Acknowledgments

INTEROCEANIC CANAL OF COLOMBIA

FOREWORD BY PROFESSOR JOAQUÍN CATALÁ ALÍS, PH.D, CIVIL ENGINEERING

A new Interoceanic Canal, a new modification of a strip in a corner of our planet, a new challenge for the most beautiful country on Earth! A necessary utopia? A work for the future, with future?

We write this prologue, feeling very honored by the fact that CANATCOL, its executives, "thought of us" to preface the book. It is for us an audacity that we assume for the love of Colombia, for the love of its people.

This prologue is a reflection from the outside, trying to be devoid of the subjectivity that closeness, friendship and interest can produce. And we do it overwhelmed, alarmed, almost scared, by reading the dedication of the book: "*Dedicated to Santa María del Darién, to intercede for the Children of Chocó who die due to hunger and malnutrition.*" Terrible to know it, terrible not to have known it before, terrible that, perhaps, most Colombians do not know it!

This is the reason, the central argument, in our opinion, of the book: people who are born, live and die in Chocó. We have been privileged witnesses, in recent years, of congresses, meetings, conversations, about the Colombia Canal, and always we have checked what moves the people who so selflessly are advancing this process. What makes them work in this wonderful utopia?   It is not money, not fame, but the social, the human, the concern to remove their people from a situation they do not deserve.

We join the Choco*anos* and the authors of this book, with pleasure and honored, to contribute, with that same philosophy, with that same concern, with those same purposes, our humble words now and our possible technical and management support maybe later.

It is not a new idea, the authors of the book explain in their first eight chapters, as they show us the history of previous studies, of wonderful ideas based on projects or designs made with very scarce and unreliable media; also the history of legal decisions, laws, decrees, which were not enacted then, and give an administrative, legal, and technical perspective to times without computers, without ICTs, without GIS, without many other advances of the current technologies.

One of the key words that this dissertation embodies is "opportunity". Yes, the opportunity to take advantage of these advances, that allow, technically, to avoid or minimize the effects, for example, of surprises like the constant and unexpected landslides of the mountain of La Culebra in the Panama Canal, whose equivalent would be the mountain range of the *Serranía de Baudó*, in Chocó. Modern techniques such as laser must be used due to the hardness of the materials to be excavated.

Another opportunity for implementation, as the authors tell us of older ship dimensions, even exceeding those acceptable for the recent expansion of the Panama Canal; or about other similar projects or ideas, such as a canal in Nicaragua (a new – old idea); or about the response to another apparent need, specially to create more ports in Colombia, given Colombia has been gifted with coasts both in the Pacific and Atlantic Oceans.

This book aims to lay the foundations for the future of the Colombia Canal, on the technical side and, somewhat, to its management process, by addressing the big issues to the resolution of all the problems. It is one of the bets from the book: the future of this great project.

Also, this book aims to transform this utopia into a real project with guarantees: that be economically and financially viable; that also be viable in the technical and environmental aspects; and, of course, this project of infrastructure will provide the change in the social conditions of life in the Colombian Chocó by alluding to the resources that will create jobs, education and the services needed to maintain a worthy existence.

And finally, this book senses the geopolitically aspect due to its national and supranational character. For example, it could involve the Panama Canal authorities, its partners in the United States of America, and also the interests of entities of Colombia affected because of the changes in the transport and communications strategy that the Colombia Canal would it imply.

In our humble opinion, these are the keys to the success of a project of this size. It did not scare Ferdinand of Lesseps when he proposed the Suez Canal project or the Panama Canal project. The last one failed for well-known reasons. It did not frighten the Americans either, or the Government of the United States of America, (for geopolitical reasons), to the point of channeling the financing through the Government itself, without limited budget, according to the chronicles.

We will not worry about the technical aspects only, but propose solutions to all the problems raised: how to avoid or minimize the clearing of the mountain range; the design of the final route of the canal; or if two ports are necessary, one in each ocean; whether or not some floodgates are needed, at least in the Pacific Ocean side. The book does get into these issues, which are the basis, as we said, of the process.

But, where are the "future lines" of this magnificent work going? The great parameters mentioned above (the Social, the Environment, the Economic - Financial, the Geopolitical, even the Technical) could not seriously condition for decisions that can be made a priori? Shouldn't we go step by step, delving into all these parameters, from the general to the particular, at the same time, before the crucial decisions are made?

Another objective of the book, another argument to support its need, its edition, is the dissemination of the subject in itself; of the problems that the canal tries to solve and those that can generate and how to alleviate them; from the benefits for the Chocoanos, for all Colombia, that can represent this great work; its enormous social impact, immediate and future. And disclosure maybe necessary to answer an initial question of any investigative process (and the book, in a way, does): who is interested in this topic, in the construction and operation of a canal of Colombia? The State? the Government? or the local authorities? The Colombian Universities? Colombians in general? Chocoanos in particular?

This disclosure is essential to properly cement the process, to have the necessary social support, in its broadest sense, so as not to have to "sell" the idea to external agents, possibly strangers to Colombia and to the Chocoanos. We estimate that this is one of the premises of CANATCOL: that the Colombian Canal belongs to the Chocoanos, that it is for the Chocoanos and by the Chocoanos. Could it be that way?

The text recreates the prehistory of the canal, as said, in its first chapters. The following pose, first, a statement of reasons, of justification of the project; also, the legal, including a proposed legislation with a character markedly realistic and practical; the technical, with pre layouts, designs and solutions; the financial, opening diverse possibilities to analyze and specify; the steps to follow, in broad strokes; the future in definitive. According to words we take from Alberto Peñín, "A text to make us reflect, but also to imagine, to make us dream… with our feet on the ground, in reality and on the slopes above mentioned".

In short, words like the future (that of Colombia, that of its inhabitants), opportunity (for the most socially depressed area of Colombia), viability (social, technical, economic - financial and environmental), legality (current and proposed), commitment (from CANATCOL and what it is expected of the Colombian authorities), are the keys of the book and the ultimate goal: the design, the construction and the administration of the Colombia Interoceanic Canal, an attainable utopia.

JOAQUÍN CATALÁ ALÍS

Doctor Engineer of Roads, Canals and Ports

Professor, Department of Construction Engineering and Civil Engineering Projects

Polytechnic University of Valencia, Spain.

e.mail: jcatala@cst.upv.es

Whatsapp: +34.680.547918

Skype: ximo.catala.alis

INTRODUCTION

With the news we heard from Colombia in 2012 that indigenous children had committed suicide due to hunger, we have investigated what could be done other than simply putting a small cure to the situation. New generations of Colombians are unaware of the hidden treasure that lies abandoned and forgotten by all. The remote Chocó, which does not have pure water even though it rains 12.5 meters (41 feet) a year, has no electricity despite having 1,000 rivers, has no infrastructure despite having rich gold and platinum mines, is starving amid wealth.

For this reason, it has been thought of reviving the megaproject discussed for more than 160 years, of opening the way to create a Canal that links the Pacific and Atlantic Oceans, through the fourth largest river in the world, the Atrato. This mega project, we think would instigate the development of one of the richest areas in Colombia's natural resources, but where poverty also abounds.

We translated the book by William Kennish and Frederick M. Kelley, "Interoceanic Canal of Colombia: Discovery and Exploration of the Interoceanic Canal Via Atrato-Truandó" (1855) from English to Spanish so that Colombians can learn about the explorations that were made in the 19th century.

In our research, we have found more than 300 bibliographical references. One of the most important, has been the collection of 7 volumes of the American Commission for the Interoceanic Canal (Volume 5) published in 1970 where it is concluded that the most acceptable route they discovered was Route # 25 to make an Interoceanic Canal that goes from Curiché, Chocó at 7 ° north latitude, to the mouth of the Atrato River through the Tarena mouth in the Municipality of Unguía.

That is the treasure of Colombia: an interoceanic route at sea-level, without locks for new sea giants that carry containers from one ocean to another. A project of this magnitude would create foreign exchange tickets that would allow the construction of the work to be paid in a short time.

This mega project will be a development pole, which will create an industrial, commercial, free zone; will generate enough resources for health, education and will allow the attention to basic children's needs to end child mortality, five times higher in all Colombia. Also, it will improve the nutrition of children to end the problem of malnutrition and childhood anemia.

The will of the Colombian leaders and communities is necessary to allow the development of this area, in the most enviable corner of South America.

According to figures from the Colombian Mining Information System (SIMCO) of the Ministry of Mines, Chocó produces 47% of Colombia's gold; In 2013 it produced 1,792,242.96 ounces of gold and 59,019.12 ounces of platinum. We wonder where is all that wealth? This amounts to more than one billion dollars, however the Chocó lives amid absolute misery.

The statistics of the various Colombian official entities indicate the following data in Chocó:

1. Maternal mortality 366: 100,000. The highest in the Western Hemisphere.

2. Infant mortality 100: 1000 (DANE).

3. Children from 5 to 10 years commit suicide due to hunger (RCN, 2012).

4. Malnutrition and childhood anemia 73% (ICBF).

5. Unemployment 28.5% (DANE), according to the Bishops of Chocó, the figure is

   60%.

6. Infrastructure is minimal.

7. Twelve hospitals do not have water or electricity in Chocó.

8. Poverty rate 67% (DANE).

The data encourages endless violence in Colombia, which continuously displaces the inhabitants, in a war that has lasted 50 years. To add to this desolate image of our beautiful country, the State continues the "chemical and biological warfare" in which illegal crops are aspersed from planes, hurting the farmers of Colombia. The only country in the world that allows what they euphemistically call "spraying" which is prohibited by article # 81 of the 1991 Constitution of Colombia.

1. DEFINITIONS AND HISTORICAL SUMMARY

Canal, word derived from the Latin "Canalis", according to the Larousse dictionary means: "River, excavated or artificial channel, which by means of locks, allows ships to save the differences in level. Maritime channel, which makes two seas communicate with each other like the Panama Canal ". Webster says: "Artificial waterway for navigation, irrigation, etc."

The first definition would exclude sea-level canals that do not need locks to pass from one ocean to another. "In engineering, a construction channel for the transport of fluids - usually used for water - is called a channel and, unlike pipes, it is open to the atmosphere. They are also used as artificial waterways." [Wikipedia]

Nor does natural waterways such as the English Channel that separates the British Isles from Europe come into the definition. There they crossed the Roman galleys to invade that country. At the beginning of the second millennium, William the Conqueror crossed the canal with his Normans. On June 6, 1944, a million soldiers crossed the route to reach the beaches of Normandy and defeat Hitler's National Socialist army in World War II.

The 1976 km (1227 miles) Grand Canal of China was built in the year 605 of our era. The ancient Egyptians linked the Mediterranean with the Red Sea. The waters of the Nile were used to irrigate the fields, but the desert was also excavated in time immemorial to communicate the two seas. Fernando de Lesseps opened the Suez Canal in 1869 and began construction of the Panama Canal in 1870.

In 1513 the King of Spain on the appointment card of the Governor of Panama Pedrarias Dávila, recommended exploring the region. He didn't know that Vasco Núñez de Balboa had discovered the South Sea in that same year. And Don Juan de Castellanos says, "And towards Panama I lead the bow, to the South Sea, which Balboa discovered."

In March 2012, Radio Cadena Nacional de Colombia presented the news about children from Chocó from 5 to 10 years who committed suicide due to hunger. Given this tragic situation we decided to investigate the problem and dedicate efforts to find solutions to solve this humanitarian crisis, denounced by the Catholic Bishops in 2014, and again by Monsignor Juan Carlos Barreto, Bishop of Quibdó in July, 2019, and confirmed by the Ombudsman for the United Nations.

<https://www.youtube.com/watch?v=mD87t3iyWMY>.

Due to the strategic situation of Chocó, which has coasts in the two oceans, and countless natural resources, it was thought whether the development of the infrastructure could solve the humanitarian crisis. One of these infrastructure projects, to unite the two oceans is the Interoceanic Canal of Colombia.

We found more than three hundred articles, and studies of all aspects of the Canal Zone of Colombia. Nineteen theses of the Superior School of War of Colombia: one of them from Colonel Luis Laverde Goubert, 1956, which won the Lorenzo Codazzi Award, which is the Canal prefeasibility study. In total there are 600 typed pages that are unpublished.

In this publication we wish to present the information that we have been compiling on the Colombian Canals from the Canal del Dique excavated in the middle of the 17th century to the studies for the construction of the Interoceanic Canal of Colombia at sea-level for Ultra Large Container Ships (known by the English acronym ULCS).

The length of the new locks of the Panama Canal (2015) of 366 meters long does not allow the passage of ULCS of more than 400 meters of length. These ocean giants will be 85% of the World Merchant Fleet in 2030.

The construction of the new Canal is imperative and urgent. Detailed studies of 30 possible sites for channels in America by the Commission of the United States (1970), concluded that the only possible site where a channel can be excavated at sea-level is in Colombia.

The exploration of the Colombo-American Commission of the late 1940s in which Major Luis Laverde Goubert participated, was the basis for US Law 280 of 1949.

The route of the Atrato-Truandó Canal must be modified to facilitate the navigation of the ULCS by reducing from eight to one curve of more than 110°. We consider the route between Coredó 6.93-76.98 and Unguía 8.05-77.1, 172 km, ideal. This route extends through the municipalities of Juradó, Riosucio, Unguía (Chocó) and Turbo, (Antioquia).

The owners of the Canal Zone are the Community Councils and the Indigenous Councils gathered in the Private Association "CANATCOL, AP". Two possibilities have been thought of: replacing Law 53/1984 with a new one that orders the 27 Military Engineer Battalions to build the Canal or give a concession for 30 years to one or more engineering companies that meet in consortium to repeat the studies, obtain licenses, finance, build, operate and maintain the Interoceanic Canal.

A cost of one million dollars per kilometer and toll revenues of the order of six billion dollars per year (US $ 6,000 million) are estimated. There is a background of the greatest importance: Military Engineers of the United States under the command of Colonel Russell completed the work of the Panama Canal in 1914. The Military Engineers of Egypt under President Al Si-Si expanded the Suez Canal in 2014. The United States Military Engineers have been in charge of controlling the rivers, canals and ports of United States for many years. There is also the International Water Resources Management Center (ICIC) that could provide technical assistance to Colombia.

According to personal information of the architect Hernando Vargas Rubiano to the architect Alberto Mendoza Morales (1996) there are another 10 isthmuses in Colombia where rivers could be communicated to increase inland navigation, one of the most economical methods of transportation that have been forgotten by Colombians. The channeling of the Magdalena River and the construction of locks in the Honda streams would make navigation from Girardot to Barranquilla possible. Through channels you can connect the rivers of the plains to the Orinoco and those of southern Colombia within the Amazonian trapeze.

The Canal between Tagua and Puerto Leguízamo could allow navigation between Florence on the Horteguaza River to Caquetá to connect with the Putumayo. One of its tributaries is the Cotué River (-2,8883 and -69,7333), and the Amacayacú River, the western limit of the Amacayacú Natural Park, which flows into the Amazon River.

There are isthmus between the Arauca and Cravo Norte, Meta Tomo, Tuparro, Muco, Ariari, Guaviare, Inirida, Vaupés, and Caguan rivers. Through these channels you can reach the Orinoco River.

500 years ago, Vasco Núñez de Balboa discovered the South Sea (Pacific Ocean as we call it today). Since that time there has been interest in finding a route to link the two oceans. According to Father Ramírez, the first to suggest a communication between the Gulf of San Miguel and the Atrato River, was "one such Saavedra" contemporary of Balboa. [Ramírez JE, 1967]. King Carlos V gave orders to the new Governor Pedrarias Dávila (1514) to discover the South Sea. [The King did not know that it had already been discovered in 1513 by Vasco Nuñez de Balboa]. The King wrote: "be made from the village of our Santa María del Darién, until the southern sea, three or four seats in the parts that seem most profitable in the Gulf of Urabá, to cross and trample the land from one part to the other, and where with less difficulty the People can walk, and in places that seem to be healthier, and have good waters and seats, according to the instruction you took: and the seat that is ovided to do ... in the South Sea, must be in the port that is better and more convenient for the contracting of

that gulf ".

[Letter from the Catholic King to Pedrarias Dávila, 1514. On the means of facilitating communication between the Darién coast and the South Sea, Simancas Archive, Spanish Archives Portal, Madrid.]

Canal del Dique. Fotografía Stephan Riedel. Tomada de: Banco de Occidente. *Río Grande de la Magdalena*. Bogotá, D.C., I/M Editores, 2003.

2. 17TH CENTURY:

CANAL DEL DIQUE, 1650

First Canal of the New World.

Don Juan de Castellanos, author of the longest poem in the Spanish language, wrote in his song: "And the History of Cartagena." The chronicler narrates that in the year of one thousand five hundred and thirty-three (1533) the Spanish-born Madrid conqueror of pure strain, Don Pedro de Heredia founded the New Cartagena, Cartagena de Levante, which has finally been called Cartagena de Indias. The Heroic city, the stone corralito for its powerful walls, was the most important port of the Conquest and the Colony, attacked on many occasions by pirates and by expeditions like that of Admiral Vernon who could not take Cartagena with 25,000 soldiers for the courage and tenacity of the defenders commanded by Don Blas de Lezo and the Viceroy Slavic.

At the beginning of the 17th century the Cartageneros worried about the pirates' attacks on their city began to fortify it, to build the Fort of San Felipe de Barajas and an escape route that would allow them to leave the city towards Calamar. Almost 50 years passed, when Don Pedro Zapata de Mendoza arrived as new Governor, who presented and received approval for the construction of the Canal del Dique to link the Bay of Cartagena with Calamar, port on the Magdalena River, a distance of 119 km. which has 56 meters wide and 2.40 meters minimum depth. The Franciscan clergyman, "understood in the matter", Fray Francisco de Rada, and the military engineer Juan de Somovilla Tejada were appointed to accompany the governor on site visits and give him technical assistance." They joined Maria and Matuma's swamps to allow the navigation of ships of up to a thousand tons that years later were steam driven.

In the Archive of the Indies is the file on the Canal del Dique (1647-63). [General Archive of the Indies, AGI, Santa Fe, 199]. Of which we transcribe:

"A race against time began then, because the excavation must be finished before the winter rains. The mobilization was extraordinary, since almost 2,000 men gathered between pawns, starters and officers. The work began on March 7, 1650 and they finished on August 20. According to the scribe of the Cabildo, "between 4 or 5 in the afternoon, apparently according to the sun, I saw that the people who work in the dike and new river broke the land that was in the mouth of the said dike and on the bank of the great Magdalena river, and having made it, a great water stroke entered and ran with great violence down the said new river below according to its current. " The construction had required the opening of two large ditches, one to the west, in the area of Matumilla, and another to the east, to communicate the Magdalena with the pipe. The cost was about 50,000 pesos, "so small a price that decreases the greatness of the work," according to Governor Zapata. He did not deprive himself of remembering that the land where the dike was opened belonged to the Cabildo of Cartagena, or that he had put money from his pocket, along with other "good republics". Despite this, the city had to take 10,000 pesos to fund the work. The Canal del Dique began to be used by small boats, canoes, pushpins and champagnes, which used 3 or 4 days to cross it. The Cabildo imposed various levies on the goods that were transported. The cost of freight transport, compared to the previous mixed route with canoes and mule tanks, was reduced by 50% and trade between the coast and the interior experienced a remarkable expansion. Despite this, the maintenance of the work was null, due to a combination of institutional abandonment and vested interests. Letters were sent to the Council of the Indies in which, in addition to accusing the former governor Zapata of thievery, quarrelsome and mockery of women, they questioned the utility and security of the Canal. This deteriorated rapidly, partly also because the Cabildo exploited it through a leasing system. In 1679 only the half dike was open, from Matumilla to Mahates. The only works done were small cleanings and the arrangement of bridges.

Summarizing, the Canal del Dique is an artificial channel that departs from the town of Calamar on the Magdalena River and goes out to the sea at the point called "Boca Cerrada".

The Canal del Dique was used for more than 350 years for inland navigation with very little maintenance. There were problems such as floods that were recorded in 2010 by the breaking of a section of its wall, affecting several municipalities of Bolívar and Atlántico, which caused the displacement of 100,000 families. The Government contracted the services of a Dutch and a Colombian company to do the renovation work "the approved solution consists of a 820 feet (250 m) long navigation sluice and a 197 feet (60 m) wide entrance structure in Calamar to reduce and control the entrance of water and sediments in the Canal del Dique ", Paola Andrea Vargas Rubio - of La República newspaper.

References

The Canal del Dique [PARES, Spanish Archives Portal on the Net]. Bank of the Republic (Colombia).

"Sealed agreement to finally execute the recovery works of the Canal del Dique" construction of two locks: one in Calamar and one in Puerto Badel, Metro, May 18, 2019 https://revistametro.co/2019/05/18/canal-dique-acuerdo/

The Canal del Dique 1810-1840: The Viacrucis of Cartagena www.banrepcultural.org/blaavirtual/publicacionesbanrep/.../canal.htm

Blanco Soto, P: The Canal between Barranquilla and Sabanilla / 1959.

Covo Torres, P: Outline of the History of Cartagena de Indias, Tecnar Cartagena de Indias 2012.

Herráez Sánchez de Escariche, Julia, School of Hispanic-American Studies, 1946 - Cartagena (Colombia) - 137 pages

http://books.google.com/books/about/Don_Pedro_Zapata_de_Mendoza_gobernador_d .html?id=0HBTAAAAYAAJ

Lemus, GB- 1989 Canal del Dique 1810-1840: The Viacrucis of Cartagena

www.banrepcultural.org/blaavirtual/publicacionesbanrep/.../canal.htm

El canal del Cura, Chocó

3. 18TH CENTURY:

FIRST INTEROCEANIC CANAL OF AMERICA: CURA CANAL,1778.

The first Interoceanic Canal in America was the Cura Canal, named for having been built by Gabriel Arrachateguí, a Catholic priest, miner and merchant who linked the Atrato and San Juan rivers through the Raspadura ravine in 1788. The width of the canal is only two meters, but it served to carry armament and ammunition to Cartagena in the Colombian War of Independence. This was confirmed by Humboldt: "Inside the Chocó Province, the Raspadura gorge joins the San Juan river and the Quito stream, the Andagueda river and the Ziratán river form the Atrato that flows into the Atlantic, while the San Juan goes to the Pacific.

The parish priest of Novita opened it with his faithful a canal for canoes to take cocoa from sea to sea, this is known in Europe since 1788. The distance between the two mouths is 75 leagues.

4. 19TH CENTURY:

ORDER OF SIMON BOLIVAR TO GOVERNOR OF CHOCO TO BUILD THE INTEROCEANIC CANAL IN 1820.

In 1820 Simón Bolívar ordered the Governor of the Chocó Colonel José María Cancino to build the San Pablo canal, 46 km between the Atrato and San Juan rivers. Then in 1827 Robert Stephenson, the son of George Stephenson visited Bogotá and proposed to the Liberator Simón Bolívar the construction of the Panama Isthmus railway. These dreams are still standing and all those who have studied geography in the classrooms of Colombian schools, are witnesses of that historical project that has not yet been accomplished in the last two centuries.

A short time ago we received a message from a person who said he had known about the work we are doing in Chocó and for very personal reasons he wanted to participate in this endeavor. We immediately remembered the illustrious last name of the hero of Independence of the New Granada, Liberator of Chocó, Governor of this Department and Military Chief of the Province of Cauca. We knew that Colonel José María Cancino was the son of Colonel Salvador Cancino, martyr of Independence, shot in Cartagena by Pacifier Morillo. His grandfather, the Protomedical of Santa Fe de Bogotá Doctor José Vicente Román Cancino was the first Professor of Medicine at the Universidad del Rosario in 1753 in Colombia. Colonel José María Cancino participated in the liberating deed and was Ensign in the Battle of Boyacá. He was the director of the music band and performed the Winning March to celebrate the victory. He was awarded by the Liberator Simón Bolívar with the Cross of Boyacá; after his promotion to Colonel, he was head of the troops that moved to Chocó to liberate that region of New Granada. In that position, Bolivar sent him the following office:

DOCUMENT 6631.

OFFICE OF JOSÉ GABRIEL PÉREZ TO THE GOVERNOR OF CHOCÓ CORONEL JOSÉ MARÍA CANCINO, dated in Popayán on February 11, 1822 whereby he tells him that the Liberator wishes to open the canal of the Isthmus that separates the two rivers. Popayán, February 12, 1822.

To the Governor of Chocó, Colonel José María Cancino:

(1 <http: // www.archivodellibertador.gob.ve/ writings / search engine / spip.php? Article 5619 # nb1>).

"I have had the honor of receiving the Office of Your Excellency of January 25 last in San Pablo and to give account of it to H.E. the Liberator, who has served to prevent me from telling Your Excellency to trace the Canal through the part of the Isthmus that separates the two rivers and has only three miles in a land of gravel and clay. To use pikes and shovels to allow access towards other villages where the Canal can also be opened; commissioned by Your Excellency to Jamaica the instruments necessary for this operation, which will be paid on behalf of the Government, then it would be for the month of October in Chocó and it is determined to execute the useful company of communicating the two seas; and he hopes that by the time he arrives, Your Excellency, he will have done what is discussed above and will have taken certain news, accurate reports, shortcomings and circumstances of how much is necessary for this important work, consulting with the practitioners of the places. God bless you."

(1 <http: // www.archivodellibertador.gob.ve/ writings / search engine / spip.php? Article 5619 # nb1>).

JOSÉ GABRIEL PÉREZ

* From a copier of the Liberator Archive. O'Leary Section, Volume XIX, page 135 to 136. <http: // www.archivodellibertador.gob.ve/ writings / search / spip.php? article 5619 # nh1>]

We do not know the reasons why the order of Bolivar could not be fulfilled, but the message of the Liberator has been passed from hand to hand among the descendants of Colonel Cancino who died at his estate in Tuluá, Valle. Now Don Fernando Cancino Restrepo has asked us to give a report on the Interoceanic Canal of Chocó and we will gladly collaborate with that distinction.

5. 19TH CENTURY:

Humboldt, Paris 1811 (LOC 2017

ALEXANDER VON HUMBOLDT

With the academic edition of Alberto Gómez Gutiérrez, the monumental work "Humboldtiana Neogranadina" was presented on August 30, 2018 at the National Museum of Colombia. Congratulations to the editors of the work of Baron von Humboldt, who pursued the proposal of the Interoceanic Canal to join the Atlantic and

Pacific Oceans by the Darién isthmus, the only place in America where you can make a canal at sea-level.

Baron Alexander von Humboldt in his book "Political Essay on the Kingdom of New Spain" translated from French and published in London in 1811 said: "To the southeast of Panama along the coast of the Pacific Ocean, there is a small port and Cupica Bay. The name of this bay has become famous in the Kingdom of New Granada for a project of a canal to link the two oceans. Cupica is 5 or 6 sea leagues from the Napipi River that flows into the Atrato. "

FREDERICK M. KELLEY

In 1855 Captain William Kennish, sponsored by Mr. Frederick M. Kelley, found the estuary of the Paracuchichi River at 7° north latitude on the Pacific coast. It crossed the Baudo range and proposed the construction of two tunnels three miles long to reach the Atlantic slope through the Nerqua, Truandó and Atrato Rivers.

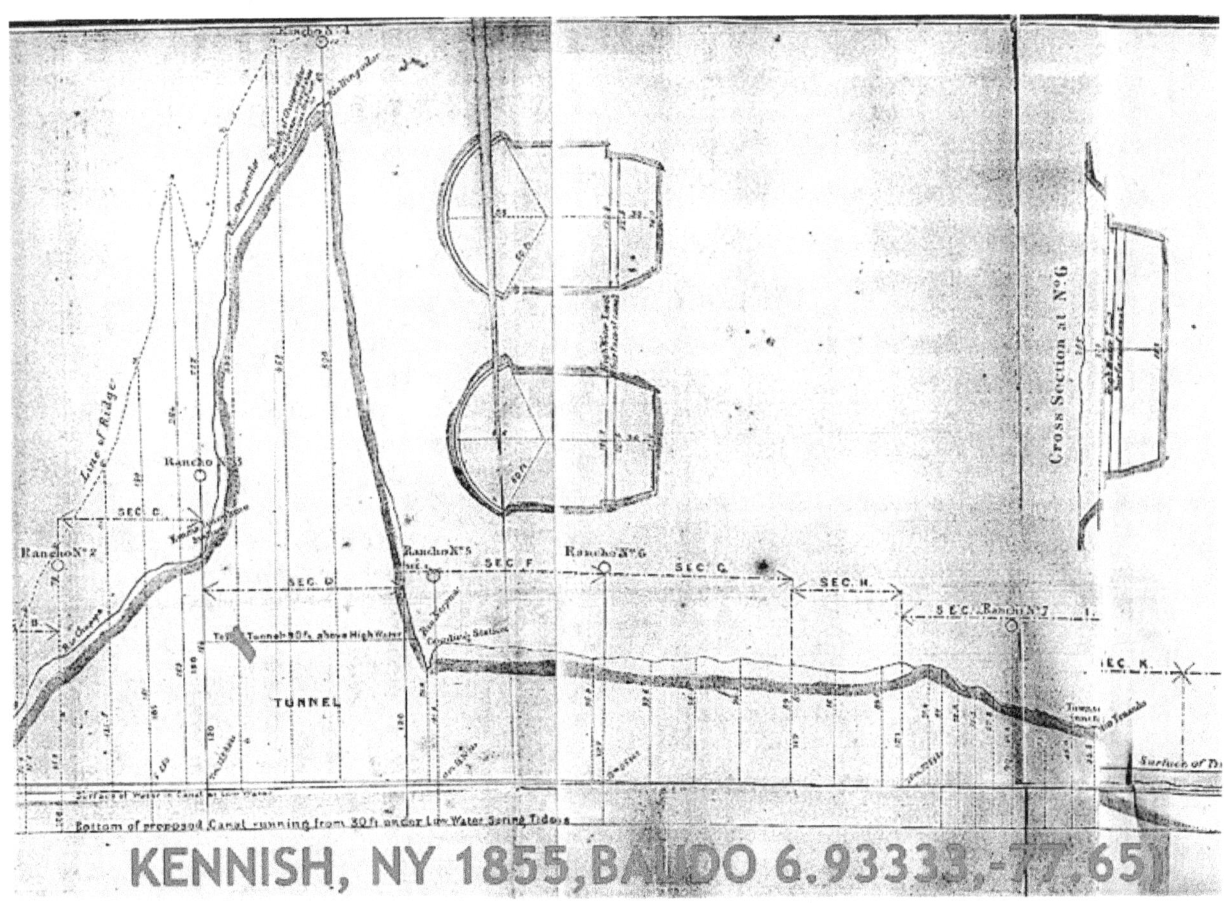

Since the discovery of the Atrato-Truandó route by William Kennish in 1854, a myriad of studies has been made. Two years later Lieutenant Nathaniel Michler was sent by the US Government to confirm Kennish's findings. He made the tour in the opposite direction and presented his report to the US Congress in 1861 (Google Books).

REPORT

OF

THE SECRETARY OF WAR,

COMMUNICATING,

In compliance with a resolution of the Senate, Lieutenant Michler's (report of his survey for an interoceanic ship canal near the Isthmus of Darien.)

FEBRUARY 15, 1861.—Read and ordered to lie on the table. Motion to print referred to the Committee on Printing.
FEBRUARY 16, 1861.—Committee discharged. Ordered to be printed.

WAR DEPARTMENT, *February* 12, 1861.

SIR: I have the honor to transmit herewith a communication from the chief topographical engineer, accompanied by the report of Lieutenant Michler, of his survey for an interoceanic ship canal near the Isthmus of Darien, called for by a resolution of the Senate of June 5, 1860.

Very respectfully, your obedient servant,

J. HOLT,
Secretary of War.

Hon. J. C. BRECKINRIDGE,

Frederick Medard Kelley (1822-1905), Banker of Wall Street, New York, sponsored seven expeditions to find the way for the Interoceanic Canal at sea-level in the Darién region, in the second half of the 19th century.

Federick Medard Kelley was born in Carmel, Putnam County, in New York State on July 26, 1822. His parents were Ebenezer Kelley and Huldah Foster. His father was the owner of Carmel Bank, Putnam County, New York, where his uncle Francis Edward Kelley (1825-1864) worked as a cashier.

Frederick M. Kelley contracted his first nuptials in 1850 with Emma Josephine Gardner (1832-1879) had no offspring. Second nuptials with Laura Ann. They were the parents of Francis Eugene Kelley and Robertino Kelley (1858-1949). His address was 153 W. 45th street, New York.

In 1842-43 he studied at the Amenia Seminary in New York. His first job was as a Drew Robinson Bank employee. Mr. Drew was also born in Carmel, New York.

He subsequently devoted himself to business in the Wall Street stock market and amassed a great fortune.

In the 1855 Census he was 33 years old, he lived in the home of his father-in-law William R. J. Gardner Ward 3, New York, NY with his wife Emma J. Kelley, 23.

Frederick M. Kelley read the publications made by Alexander Von Humboldt in the early nineteenth century about the communication of the two oceans and the Atrato River and dedicated his life and his fortune to pursue that ideal.

Kelley was one of the forerunners of the explorations and studies to find the most suitable route to unite the Atlantic and the Pacific through the Darién Isthmus. In 1850, General Hilario López, President of Colombia, granted Mr. Kelley permission to travel to the Province of Cauca to which the current Department of Chocó belonged.

On March 1, 1880 the New York Merchants offered a Gala banquet at the Delmónico Hotel in honor of Ferdinand de Lesseps. 250 people attended and distinguished speakers included Mr. Frederick M. Kelley of New York, who informed the audience of the seven expeditions he sponsored to explore the interoceanic route at sea-level.

THE

PRACTICABILITY AND IMPORTANCE

OF A

SHIP CANAL

TO CONNECT THE

ATLANTIC & PACIFIC OCEANS.

WITH A HISTORY OF THE ENTERPRISE

From its first Inception to the Completion of the Surveys.

INCLUDING THE INSTRUCTIONS FROM F. M. KELLEY, ESQ., TO WILLIAM
KENNISH, ESQ., CIVIL ENGINEER—REPORT OF MR. KENNISH'S SURVEY,
WITH ACCOMPANYING PLATES, AND A PAPER UPON THE THEORY
OF THE TIDES—CONFIRMATORY REPORT OF E. W. SERRELL,
ESQ., CONSULTING ENGINEER—AND AN ESSAY UPON
THE IMPORTANCE OF THE CANAL IN ITS RELATIONS
TO THE COMMERCE OF THE WORLD.

NEW-YORK:
GEORGE F. NESBITT & CO., PRINTERS AND STATIONERS,
Corner Pearl and Pine Streets.
1855.

The seven expeditions sponsored by Frederick M. Kelley included the following:

1. In 1852 John C. Trautwine, Engineer of Philadelphia traveled the route of the Atrato-San Juan rivers, surveyed and subsequently published a map of the region.

2. In 1853 Mr. Kelley sent an expedition commanded by Mr. Mark B. Porter

3. In 1853 Mr. Kelley sent a second expedition commanded by Colonel Lane.

4. In 1854 the expedition was commanded solely by Colonel Lane.

5. In 1855 Captain William Kennish discovered the Atrato-Truandó route 130 miles (209 km) for a canal 200 feet (60 m) wide and 30 feet (9 m) deep. In 1854 Mr. Frederick M. Kelley gave precise instructions to Captain William Kennish, a civil engineer, to find a port at 7° north latitude on the Pacific Ocean coast. Captain Kennish traveled at the end of 1854, toured the coast of New Granada from Punta Ardita until he found the Paracuchichi estuary, seven miles away from Coredó. The expedition continued along this river until it reached the dividing line of the Pacific and Atlantic slopes. He continued his journey through the Hingador river to reach the Nerqua valley, continued along this river until reaching the Truandó and navigated through it to the Atrato to reach it at the mouth of the Gulf of Urabá.

The eminent explorer considered viable the construction of a canal at sea-level without locks to join the two oceans. He recommended two three-mile tunnels to cross the Baudo range. In 1858 US President James Buchanan commissioned Lieutenant Nathaniel Michler and 22 scientists, who confirmed the findings of Captain Kennish and reported to the US Congress in 1861.

6. In 1863 the expedition was co-sponsored by Mr. Cyrus Butler and Mr. Like T. Merritt, commanded by Mr. Norman Rude, who explored the Gulf of San Blas region.

7. In 1864 Mr. McDougall found a 30-mile interoceanic route through the Bayamon River and proposed a tunnel 7 to 10 miles long.

The first expedition was commanded by Philadelphia Engineer John C. Trautwine in 1852. He toured the Atrato and San Juan Rivers and drew up a map of the region. He did not find the Canal del Cura excavated by Presbyter Gabriel Arrachategui, Parish priest of Novita, with his parishioners in 1778. Tomás Castrillón Muñoz wrote in 1964 that the reason for having done this work had been a dispute of boundaries between the Mosquera and Salinas families. The Cura Canal connects the Atrato and San Juan Rivers through the Raspadura ravine. It is two meters wide and allows the passage of canoes. It was the first Interoceanic Canal in America.

The following expeditions on behalf of Kelley, were carried out by Colonel Lane and Porter during the years 1853 and 1854. Lane, who knew something about the Truandó River in Quibdó, included in his study a map of the Chocó province dated at 1856. The study is entitled: "Atlantic-Pacific Canal Company; Report on the Cartographic Survey of the Atrato, Pató and Baudó Rivers." (New York, 1856).

In late 1854 Frederick M. Kelley sponsored the fifth expedition under the command of Captain William Kennish. It crossed the Isthmus of Panama (the Panama Railroad began operating on January 28, 1855). He arrived in Panama City where he acquired a ship to take him along the Pacific coast to the south of Humboldt Bay 7° north latitude, in the Curiché River estuary that Kennish nominated as "Kelley inlet". At the beginning of 1855, he climbed the Baudo range, which separates the ocean from the valley of the Truandó River, a tributary of the Atrato that flows into the Atlantic Ocean.

On March 3, 1857 the Congress of the United States passed the following law: "It is decreed that the Secretaries of War and Navy are authorized under the direction of the President to employ the Army and Naval officers that are necessary in order to explore and verify the work already done on a boat canal near the Darién, to connect the waters of the Pacific and the Atlantic by the Atrato and Truandó Rivers, provided that the costs do not exceed $ 25,000, which are appropriated here for this purpose with treasure money that has not been appropriated otherwise." Signed by US President James Buchanan.

This route was confirmed by the mission commanded by Lieutenant Nathaniel Michler and 22 scientists who began the tour by entering the mouth of the Atrato River in the Atlantic Ocean in 1858. The report was presented to the Congress of that country and published in 1861. That year the Civil War began, and as a result, the project was archived and forgotten.

In 1856, Kelley visited Europe, met with Alexander von Humboldt, and went to England to present the project to Queen Victoria. He spoke at the Royal Geographic Society chaired by Robert Stephenson and was awarded the Telford Gold Medal. This Medal is the highest prize awarded by the British Institution of Civil Engineers (ICE) for an article, or a series of articles. It is worth noting that Mr. Kelley was not an engineer but a banker. He wrote several brochures and articles about the explorations in English and French. In 2014 the Digital Library of the National University of Colombia published the translation into Spanish of Frederick M. Kelley's 1855 book by Gómez and Baldwin.

Then, Mr. Kelley went to France to obtain the cooperation of those countries. Emperor Napoleon III offered to finance a third of the costs of the construction of the Canal, which was not accepted. After his return to New York in 1861, the Civil War broke out that would last until 1865.

For many years, Frederick M. Kelley devoted all his time and fortune to the promotion of the company. Two other expeditions were sent to the Province of Panama in 1863, when Norman Rude found the route of the Gulf of San Blas.

In 1864 A. Mc Dougal went to the San Blas Gulf and the Bayano river. The distance between the two pipes is 30 miles and he declared a 7 to 10-mile-long tunnel would be needed to connect them.

Mr. Kelley was in Washington in 1866 conferring with Admiral Davis on the Interoceanic Canal. He mentioned the Interoceanic Canal to Congress where they presented their work. It is said of Frederick M. Kelley that "he produced more intelligible information towards the solution of this problem, of such great importance to the commercial and political interests of the world, than what had been given so far." His research and experience gave him a recognized authority on this subject, and few men have had a broader and more precise knowledge of all matters related to the interoceanic canals. "

"For several years, Frederick M. Kelley, a Wall Street banker held the concession now owned by the French Company; he spent his private fortune of one hundred and twenty thousand dollars in the promotion of the company, to which he contributed his energy and experience" (Kelley, 1859).

Ernesto Guhl (1915-2000) in the biography of Agustín Codazzi wrote: "Frederick M. Kelley devoted himself for almost ten years to the question of the canal, with immense energy but also with many mistakes." Later he confessed: "When, in 1851, I began to study the scientific history and geographical contours of Central America, I ignored much of what had been done and written in the past and, of course, I could not know of the valuable data that has accumulated since then."

See "Kelley, The Union of the Oceans by Ship-Canal Without Locks Via the Atrato Valley [For the Transit of Ships, by the Way of the Atrato Valley] (New York, 1859), P. 5.

At the 1900 census, Mr. Kelly was 78 years old, had lost all his fortune and lived in a residence for the elderly and widowed in New York. He died in 1905 and is buried in Kelley Cemetery in Carmel, N.Y.

His obituary says: "The death of Mr. Kelley." Putnam Courier County Journal dated December 8, 1905. "Frederick M. Kelley, one of Carmel's leading men sent throughout the world, died in New York on Sunday night at 83, leaving two children, Frederick Eugene Kelley who lives in Saratoga, and Robertino Kelley lives in Toledo, Ohio. He was buried in Kelley Cemetery on Wednesday in the family plot. His death closely followed that of his sister Mrs. Mullan J. Cole. Leaves one brother, Thomas FR Kelley and two sisters Mrs. Hopkins and Mrs. Kelley, in the old house of Carmel Village. "

References

Ammen, D. The Interoceanic Ship Canal Meeting at Chickering Hall, December 9, 1879. The Proposed Interoceanic Ship Canal across Nicaragua. J Am Geographical Society New York 1879; 11: 113-152.

Bankers Magazine 1863-1864; 18 (13) Smith Romans, New York, NY.

Beers, "Commemorative Biographical Record: p. 971. New York State, Census, 1855.

Guhl, Ernesto, 1915-2000, Schumacher, Hermann, A: Codazzi, A Forger of Culture. http://www.banrepcultural.org/blaavirtual/geografia/codaz/codaz11.ht

"Pedigree Resource File," database, FamilySearch (https://familysearch.org/ark:/61903/2:2:941L-Y4H: accessed 2014-12-11), entry for Frederick M. Kelley, submitted by lbarrett2764472.

Kennish, W. CE; Kelley, FM. Esq. Map of the Isthmus of and Valley of the Atrato, Showing the Interoceanic River Aqueduct, Sheet VI, 1853, J. Royal Geographic Soc, 26.

Kelley, Frederick M. On the Junction of the Atlantic and Pacific Oceans, and the Practicability of a Ship Canal without Locks, by the Valley of the Atrato. Ed by Charles Manby, London 1856.

Kelley, Frederick M. On the Junction of the Atlantic and Pacific Oceans, and the Practicability of a Ship Canal without Locks. London: Printed by W. Clowes and sons, 1856.

Kelley, F. On the practicability of uniting the Atlantic and Pacific Oceans by the Atrato and Truandó Rivers. 1855 (Translation by Jaime Gómez González and Claudia Gómez Baldwin).

Kelley, F.M. Explorations Through the Valley of the Atrato River to the Pacific Ocean, in Search of a Route for a Ship Canal. J. Geograph Soc London, 1856; 26: 174-182.

Kelley, Frederick M. Projet d'un canal maritime sans écluses between l'océan Atlantique et l'océan Pacifique à l'aide des rivers Atrato et Truandó, Par F.M. Kelly from New York, précédé d'une introduction, avec une carte sur les différents communication projets interocéanique proposés jusqu'à ce jour; by M. V.A. Malte-Brun; et suivi d'une lettre by M. Le Baron Alexander de Humboldt. Extrait des nouvelles annales des Voyages Janvier 1857 Paris. Arthus Bertrand editeur. Libraire de la Société de Geography, 21 Rue Hautefeuille, 1857.

Kelley, Frederick M. Projet d'un canal maritime sans écluses between l'océan Atlantique et l'océan Pacifique à l'aide des rivers Atrato et Truandó, Société de Géographie Bulletin 1857; 14:75.

Kelley, Frederick M. The Union of the Oceans by Ship Canal without Locks, Via the Atrato Valley. New York, Harper & Brothers Publ. Franklin Square 1859.

Lane, James C. Report of James C. Lane on the practicability of uniting the Atlantic and Pacific Oceans by the Atrato and Truandó Rivers. New York 1855.

Annals Nouvelles des Voyages 1857; 15: 109

Malte-Brun, VA. Du projet de communication interocéanique par l'isthme de Darien. Societe de Geographie Bulletin 1857; 13: 479.

"ADDRESS OF MR. KELLEY." New York Times (1857-1922): 2. Mar 02, 1880. ProQuest. Web. 2 Jan. 2015.

ADDRESS OF MR. KELLEY (1880, Mar 02). New York Times (1857-1922) http://ezproxy.fau.edu/login?url=http://search.proquest.com/docview/93824314?accountid=10902

Courtesy of Mr. Ken Frankel, Head, Reference & Instructional Services. HE. Wimberly Library, Florida Atlantic University, Boca Raton, Florida, USA.

The National Encyclopedia of American Biography Vol 11 JT White 1901

Notes

Drew, Daniel (1797-1879) of Carmel, NY established in New York the banking firm of the Drew, Robinson & Co. He founded the Drew Ladies Seminary of Carmel and the Drew Theological seminary of Madison, NJ.

New York State Census, 1860 Carmel. Ebenezer Kelley 60 NY farmer; Francis E. 35 NY banker.

Ebenezer, Kelley President of the Bank of Commerce, Carmel, NY. Cashier Francis E. Kelly, Capital $ 87,800 (The Bankers Magazine, Volume 18) Francis Edward Kelley, (b. April 11, 1825; d. Oct. 31, 1864).

New York State, Census, 1900 (Home for old men and aged couples widowed he was 78). At the 1900 census, he was 78 years old and lived in a residence for the elderly and widowers in New York. (Ancestry Library Edition).

Kelley's book was known by Agustín Codazzi and by the father of Colombian Geography: General Francisco Javier Vergara and Velasco, but since then it had been hiding in foreign libraries until recently when the Google Company put it digitally in its book section.

This information arrives of a canal without locks in Colombian territory, which can be done, as Kennish proposed, crossing the Serranía del Baudó with two tunnels for the passage of ships. The distance to travel is only 26 kilometers that separate the Pacific Ocean from the rivers of the Atlantic slope.

This project, which requires the highest priority of the President of Colombia, was approved by law 53 of 1984. About 300 articles have been written on the subject and unfortunately, no one has worried about making it happen. Now that the first centenary of the inauguration of the Panama Canal, and the fifth centenary of the discovery of the South Sea by Vasco Nuñez de Balboa, will be completed, the steps are rapidly advancing in Nicaragua to make the canal through that country, where they will need 17 pairs of locks and it is in volcanic territory, which destroyed Managua in 1931 and 1972.

The Interoceanic Canal of Colombia is a priority for the country. The School of Military Engineers of Colombia can make the preliminary project based on the plans raised at 1: 25,000 scale by the Agustin Codazzi Geographical Institute in 1964. They must do soil studies of the Truandó and the Serranía del Baudó that have not been done and obtain those studies already made of the Atrato River.

The members of the National Committee for the Construction of the Interoceanic Canal of Colombia have all died except for Alberto Mendoza Morales, who has just retired from the Presidency of the Geographical Society of Colombia.

The Infrastructure Institute of Colombia must proceed to obtain the studies carried out by the former Ministry of Public Works, which had to cost several million dollars. Colombia needs its Canal to join the developed world.

We wish to propose that the Gulf of Urabá port be renamed of "Santa María del Darién" and "New Granada" to the port on the Pacific. It is up to this generation to do it!

EXCERPTS FROM FREDERICK M. KELLEY'S BOOK:
INTEROCEANIC CANAL OF COLOMBIA, VIA ATRATO-TRUANDÓ, 1855

"History of the exploration of the possibility and importance of a canal for ships to connect the Atlantic and Pacific Oceans. From the beginning of the trip, including the instructions of Mr. F.M Kelley, to Mr. William Kennish, Civil Engineer.

Report of the exploration of Mr. Kennish with the corresponding plates and an article on the theory of the tides.

Confirmatory report of Mr. R.W. Serrell, Consulting Engineer and report on the importance of the canal in relation to world trade. New York, Nesbitt, 1855. Reports, etc.

Instructions to a Civil Engineer New York, November 2, 1854.

Mr. Civil Engineer William Kennish,

Dear Sir:

I am pleased to form an expedition in order to explore the route of a boat canal in New Granada. For this reason, you must head to Panama, via Asinwall, on the next ship.

In Panama, rent a boat that serves in your judgment for the best purpose and continue south along the coast in order to discover a good harbor in the vicinity of latitude 7° North.

After finding a bay that can accommodate larger ships, do a hydrographic survey of the site, noting especially if there is a need for improvements to make it a completely safe site in any circumstance.

When traveling south along the coast, carefully observe the mountain range and identify a passage in that mountain range.

From the bay (if you are lucky enough to find one) continue east towards the top of the mountain range, and look for the line where you could cut open pit, without locks, for a canal for ships to connect the ocean waters of the Pacific with the Atrato River, near its confluence with the Truandó River at latitude 7° N, 77° longitude West of Greenwich.

The explorations that have been made so far of my peculiar and others made by distinguished travelers, indicate that the highest part in that direction is very low; in order to establish the lowest step - crossing the mountain range between the waters of the Pacific slope and those of the Atlantic that flow into the Atrato river in the opposite direction of the path.

When determining the lowest point of the mountain range, proceed with your exploration. It is important that when you find and indicate roughly the direction of the path, launch a transit line and measure it carefully and trace all the irregularities of the terrain using the level in the usual way.

When you cross the dividing line, in the best place continue towards the Atrato river by the most convenient route, and then go down towards the Atlantic Ocean, continuing your direction test, currents, depth surveys, etc.

At the mouth of the Atrato, do the necessary exams to locate a port. The most important thing about this survey is to establish approximately the cost of an open cut, without locks, from ocean to ocean, with a minimum depth of thirty feet at maximum low tide and wide enough to pass two of the largest floating vessels. You will fill out the details of this exam with reference to this requirement.

All the details of your time and circumstances will allow you to record the weather, natural products of all kinds of the country. Special attention is required to assess the sanitary conditions of the region.

As this is of greater importance, you must carry all the instruments and devices you require to obtain accurate data.

Report from time to time when there is an opportunity and when you have finished, please return to New York as soon as possible.

I include letters of credit and presentation to facilitate the realization of this company.

I wish health to you and your expedition and a happy return and I trust your ability, energy and dedication.

Sincerely, F.M. Kelley.

Report of the Civil Engineer William Kennish

Mr. F. M. Kelley,

In compliance with your travel orders to the Province of Chocó, in the Republic of New Granada, South America dated November 2, 1854, to explore the route to cross the mountain range from 7° North latitude in the Pacific to 77° West longitude in Greenwich, on the Atrato river in order to locate the route for an Interoceanic Canal of ships, without locks, I have the honor to inform:

Accompanied by my first assistant, Captain Norman Rude, we embarked on the George W. Law steam bound for Asinwall on November 6, 1854 and arrived on the 14th of the same month. We crossed the Isthmus and arrived in Panama the next night where we met my second assistant Dr. RG Jameson.

December 10, 1854.- We embarked for the island of Tobago and arrived the next day. There we stopped to make the necessary repairs and modifications to the bongo that we bought for the trip along the coast towards the South.

December 13.- We set sail at 1 am from the Pearl Islands that are on our way, there was a light wind.

December 14.- We sailed all night and arrived at the town of San Miguel on the island of the same name (one of the Pearl Islands), the weather was clear and pleasant.

December 15.- In San Miguel, on the 16th, 17th and 18th we were busy on the trip from the Pearl Islands to Bocachica, the smaller of two mouths that connects the Port of Darien with the gulf. On the 18th we disembarked in Palma a town or village of five houses built of cane, located within the Port of Darién.

December 19.- At 2 pm we arrived in Chapigana and disembarked at the residence of Mr. Hossack and Mr. Nelson. Here the Mayor and the town Judge came to offer their services and to give us favorable news related to the region between the Juradó river and the Atrato river.

We were worried about a possible attack by the natives of San Blas, who loathe foreigners since the evil Virago expedition commanded by Lieutenant Strain of the United States.

The reason to visit this site was to get the help of Mr. Nelson and one or two expert sailors on the Pacific coast between the Gulf of San Miguel and the Juradó river. Skillful pilots are required for this trip, as the coast is rocky and steep, there are numerous reefs, cliffs and strong currents. At noon the thermometer marked 82° F.

December 22.- We hired two sailors one for the entire trip, the other only to Garachina. Mr. Nelson also agreed to join us. Our chef defected but was returned by the Mayor. We returned from Chapiganá and Palma in the afternoon and found the tidal current very strong.

December 23.- We left Palma for Garachina passing through Boca Chica; We crossed this narrow and important step, we went to Garachina and arrived at 5:30 pm. Here we knew that it was impossible to get sailors until after Christmas, so we were in that place until the 27th.

December 24.- We took the altitude, etc. to set the length of Garachina.

December 27.- We hired a pilot and another to replace the one who left us in Garachina. In Garachina we noticed a high mountain range, one immediately behind the town, it ascends to 3,000 feet. From this point the mountain range continues south following the coast to Puerto Piñas, where there is not a small decrease in height.

December 28.- We went to the sea to surround Cabo Garachina. Fearing not to have enough water on board, we stopped at Puerto Escondido, a small boat port very inaccessible, with a narrow mouth through which there is an intense current that swells and forms large waves. After anchoring inside the harbor, we found excellent water and spent a magnificent night in the hammocks hanging from the trees.

December 29.- We embarked again with a soft and uncertain wind that forced us to anchor all night. There are few sites in this latitude of the Pacific where there is a good place to anchor. The coast to Garachina is rocky and with little beach. The hills start from the seashore to the highest peaks and are covered with dense forests, rarely crossed by humans. This is true of the entire coast from Punta Garachina to Puerto Piñas and from there to Punta Ardita. Except for Puerto Piñas, in this coastal region there is no other anchorage sufficiently deep for larger vessels, only for small cabotage vessels. Puerto Piñas, however, is the exception, it is larger and worth describing as we will do later.

December 30.- We arrived a mile and a half away from the entrance of Puerto Piñas, but we had to anchor due to the cross winds, dangerous situation. We were exposed to the hangover that threatened to throw us towards the beach.

December 31.- We raised anchors at dawn and after four hours of fighting against the current, we entered Puerto Piñas, where there are several loose rocks that mark the position of the port very well.
We entered the port at 8 am and sailed near the rocks of the northern margin until we reached the mouth of the river that flows from the high mountain range that limits the view inland. When we docked, the thermometer marked 88°F. We quickly made a refuge in the arm of sand between the river and the bay.
In the mouth, the river is two and a half miles wide and extends inwards, towards the crown of the bay for about five miles. It is surrounded by densely forested mountains and rises between 500 to 1,000 feet.
The furthest mountain range in the interior seems to be between 3,000 to 4,000 feet. The coast on both sides is cut off by bays that protect ships from the winds. They are narrow but with deep waters near the coast.
The Piñas river does not have a very important current but is subject to rapid increases, during one of which our bongo was dragged and with great difficulty we could prevent it from being taken to the bay.

The beach that surrounds the crown of the port is soft with a little pronounced decline, but due to the surf it receives strong waves that make it even dangerous to disembark even in small boats. The only place to disembark is at the mouth of the river or in several estuaries or estuaries besieged on the North and South coasts of the bay.

January 1, 1885.- We began with Dr. Jameson at 8.30 am and walked towards the crown of the port, to climb the hill. We were accompanied by the pilot and the sailors with machetes to open a path. After walking three miles on the beach we found a small waterfall of fresh water. We had breakfast and started the ascent. We carried a barometer, a thermometer and left other instruments with Captain Rude with the order to mark the hourly atmospheric pressure and temperature.
When we reached the top after ascending the steep slope of slippery terrain through the clay, we observed the instruments and found that the atmospheric pressure dropped 45-100 inch, indicating with the temperature correction, a height of 500 feet.

January 2.- We took the elevation angles to make the trigonometric calculations and confirm the height of the hill that we climbed yesterday, but the figures obtained were very sharp and therefore not satisfactory.
When ascending and measuring the hill we considered two points:

1. Test the accuracy of the barometric observation by comparing it with the trigonometric.

2. Observe the panorama from the summit. In this sense we are disappointed that the foliage is so dense that it does not allow seeing beyond a short distance. This situation is the same in all the regions visited in our tour. Therefore, all descriptions of the land from the mountains of New Granada must be received with skepticism and distrust. In our expedition to that region we have no information about the view from the summits of that country.

January 3.- In Puerto Piñas we met a resident of Juradó who gave us a magnificent description of the route between this point and the Atrato River.

January 6.- At 7 p.m. we left the port with a light and inconstant breeze. We passed seven isolated rocks that mark the southern end of the bay.

January 7.- We arrived at Punta Ardita after two days of difficult navigation, hoisting the sails when there was a breeze and anchoring when the winding stopped or there was bad weather. The coast between Puerto Piñas and Punta Ardita is rugged, rocky and dangerous. There are two important promontories, the one that is farther north is called Punta Marzo (March Point), further south is Caracoles. Near those points anchor canoes. Punta Cocalito is another one of those headlands that is six miles from Punta Ardita.
In Punta Cocalito begins a large bay where the Juradó River, the Paracuchichi and another streams flow. Here a depression of the mountain range (from thousands to hundreds of feet) where we found a route not explored until now from the Pacific to the

Atlantic. This important bay ends south on a promontory called Punta Marzo. It has an extension of at least 35 miles with a depth of 15 miles from the crown to the line between the two headlands.

The coastline has three large sandy beaches, the first of which forms the arc of a circle between Punta Ardita and the Juradó River. The second continues in a straight line from the mouth of the Juradó to that of the Paracuchichi for more than ten miles. The third extends from the last named to the mouth of the Coredó River, 15 miles. The waves of the beach break in continuous lines on these beaches. From the shore, the bottom descends in a gradual decline which allows to anchor two or three miles from the coast in waters of 10 to 30 fathoms deep. The bottom is sandy and slowly sinks away from the coast.

Outside the Ardita, Juradó and March, there are isolated rocks, but outside of this, the bay is free of obstacles.

In Coredó there is an indentation of the coast that serves as an anchorage and port where large and small ships are protected from winds 7 or 8 miles outside the mouth of the Paracuchichi, whose importance will be highlighted later. The coast between Punta Ardita and Punta Marzo deserves a special description: towards the sea is the shaded beach of coconut trees, further in there is an area of mangroves crossed by a network of natural channels where the tide rises and falls showing the communication between the rivers Juradó and Paracuchichi.

After this area, the surface slowly rises to a moderate height that does not exceed a few hundred feet. The rest of the region is covered with trees. From Coredó to Juradó and even Ardita you can't walk on the beach except when the tide is high and covers the bushes. This is the only part of the mountain range where depression is observed. The coast needs to be described in relation to the port where the canal should end. Until now we did not know of the existence of a natural port in this region except for Coredó.

"It was necessary to enter through the mouth of the Paracuchichi through the currents to reach a wide and protected bay hidden from the vision when we opted along the Paracuchichi peninsula. To summarize the narration of the events, we arrived as we said in Punta Ardita and found a small anchorage accessible only for canoes and bongos. From here our pilot showed us the entrance of the Juradó River, five miles away and said that the current was less strong to enter, however at 5 pm he changed his mind and headed through the bay of Ardita up to about one hundred yards from the mouth of the river. Here we anchored and waited for it to get dark. The depth was eight fathoms."

January 8.- We left at dawn and approached the North of the mouth of the Juradó river, but the hangover was so strong and powerful that trying to enter would be crazy. The passage is very narrow a few yards wide and can only be accessed at sometimes. There are huge rocks that break the waves into foam that rises and form rain. We moved away about a mile and then we passed the island that separates the two mouths of the Jurado which are flat at both ends and rise about 30 feet. The current was so strong that it prevented us from approaching land and when we reached the mouth of the south, we found the same problem, so we had to continue along the coast from the Juradó to find where to disembark which happened near Coredó. There we found a magnificent port at about two in the afternoon.

January 9.- Coredó is uninhabited, the hills rise sharply from the beach and are full of forests from the base to the top of the mountain. This day we conducted surveys through the port and threw a cable away from the coast and the result was an average of three fathoms. Towards the sea there is anchorage for large ships with protection against prevailing winds.

January 10.- We located the most important points between Coredó and Paracuchichi in the North direction and Northwest through the West. At night we hired the services of an expert pilot who came from Juradó to see us. We lifted anchors and crossed the mouth of the Paracuchichi.

January 11.- This morning with the expert pilot we arrived at the mouth of the river, at our anchorage in Paracuchichi. The tide as usual was high and continuous, you could only pass through the breakwaters and without wind. It was necessary to trust only the three rowers. The pilot kept the bow of the boat at a right angle to the wave line, which allowed the safe passage asking the sailors to make the greatest possible effort with voices and gestures to paddle vigorously.
We passed the big breakwaters and after the fourth we reached calm waters. A few minutes later we were floating on the surface of the river that glided smoothly through a level space covered by high-rise mangroves. From there we continued in small canoes of a native resident of the town of Eurachichi where we arrived at noon, leaving the bongo behind us to remove the mast.
We arrived at the town that has six separate houses on a smooth and extensive estuary and extends to the Northeast of the Paracuchichi, three to four miles (4-6 km) long by 250 to 500 yards (230 to 450 m) wide.
Seen from the southern part, it seems like a lake with a smooth surface protected from the winds of the Pacific by an intermediate peninsula full of coconut trees and other tropical plants that grow and tumble so densely that unless a path is followed it is impossible to cross them.
On the other side of the estuary, the vegetation is thinner, it consists of mangroves that even when they are rarely very thick, they are distinguished by the great hardness and durability of the wood, this can undoubtedly serve to make piles in any amount.
The estuary is not on any map, it is located at 6° 37' 32" N. The temperature is cool and pleasant. We did not know about diseases, except low fevers and discomfort among the natives of the neighborhood. The temperature ranges between 84° F at noon and 70° by night. The barometer between 29 35-100 and 29 42-100. The highest tide observed in Paracuchichi was 12 and a half feet (4 m) and the lowest was 10 feet 11 inches (3 m).
The survey of this estuary at low tide ranges between 2 and a half and 3 fathoms in the middle of the canal. The bottom is made of mud and sand and could easily be dredged at any depth. To the north, the river decreases in width of 20 yards (18 m) and the winds are intricate. In this direction you can sail in canoe for two thirds of the distance

to Juradó, but little by little the channel narrows, becomes less deep and finally disappears in the silt, which does not allow you to continue sailing in that direction. When the tide rises, the canoes can go much further until they find a creek that leaves one arm south of the Juradó, turning the Paracuchichi peninsula into an island. The width of this peninsula varies little along its 10 miles (16 km) long, the average distance from the estuary to the sea is 300 to 500 yards (270 to 450 m). The surface is several feet above the highest tide. The natives reported that they never remember it has been covered by water.

We did not see floating woods or similar signs of having been recently submerged. If we add the fact that in this region of the Pacific there are no storms, we reached the very important conclusion that the peninsula constitutes a permanent barrier or breakwater protecting the most beautiful and calm estuary from the sea. It seems almost made on purpose by nature to serve as a wharf or port of great importance, suitable in all aspects to serve as a terminal of the Interoceanic Canal.

The swell that I have described is a feature common to the entire Pacific coast of South America; I have noticed its presence in many places except in the places protected by the winds. It is more formidable in appearance than, especially at the bottom of the decline of the beaches. A boat with enough speed can pass safely to Paracuchichi at any time, but a bongo like the one we have is too large to be rowing and runs the risk of shipwrecking. The swell line extends towards the sea about 100 yards.

The way to connect the road with the ocean is by cutting through the peninsula to avoid the inconvenience of the waves (See plate # 3).

Before beginning the description of our route to the Atrato, I consider it necessary to point out several important conclusions that emerge from the previous narrative and observations from the coast of Garachina to the promontory of Punta Marzo:

1. The coast between Punta Garachina and Punta Ardita is steep and mountainous, the interior even more and contains only a good berth in Puerto Piña, which despite being useful in some respects, does not matter in relation to the Interoceanic Canal.

2. The depression of the mountain range observed between Punta Ardita and Punta Marzo. In this sector the region loses the mountainous character and assumes the appearance of a gradual elevation of the terrain with low elevation hills seen from a distance. This space is limited to the North by a chain of mountains in the NE direction of the neighborhood of Punta Ardita, to the South it is limited by another group of high mountains that follow a similar path and end at Punta Marzo.

3. Due to the fact that in the depression of the mountain range I have discovered an estuary, which I believe has not been described so far, of great breadth and perfectly protected with the ability to be dredged at any depth and connected to the ocean. I believe that it must be the end of the Interoceanic Canal in the Pacific Ocean and that it needs relatively little work to complete it in all the necessary aspects.

4. Because it is a safe place to anchor one or two miles from this estuary, it is also a large refuge port for Coredó that is only 7 miles (11 km) away in a straight line.

5. Because this coast almost never suffers from hurricane or cyclone attacks, on this trip and on previous occasions when I have been in this area, in open canoes with the board a few inches above the water, I have never had bad problems with weather, storms or wind gusts. There are bursts of a certain duration that can be a danger for small boats and canoes, but with the precaution of taking the sail by the hand, those bursts that last less than five minutes cannot cause danger or inconvenience.

To confirm these facts, it is important to note that the loss of a canoe or other boat on this coast is very rare despite the fact that the anchor used by sailors is only a large stone with a cable made of vines or lianas, abundant in the New Granada forests. Boats equipped in this way and at the same time driven without dexterity as they usually are, can crash into the rocks or be pushed towards the sea as can happen, but the lack of storms in this region of the coast makes it unlikely. A storm with strong winds or hurricanes can drag a ship with the anchor but this possibility does not exist in this region.

The winds of the Pacific coast are periodic: they blow from the South between March and September and from the North from September to March. Throughout the year the wind calms between 6 in the afternoon and 10 in the morning. Currently a gentle breeze begins that generally calms down or ends at 6 pm.
Consequently, a boat once towed out to sea, can depend on the breeze with which it reaches trade winds and reaches its destination in a short time. Considering all these premises, the manifest capacity of the Paracuchichi estuary, the existence of an excellent anchorage to anchor and exit to the sea and to Coredó in immediate proximity makes this estuary of the greatest importance for one of the ends of the Canal. The abundance of hardwood in the neighborhood and the absence of storms in this portion of the coast and emboldened by all the information I could get from this region and the interior of the country, I have decided to make arrangements to cross from this site to the Atrato by the lowest route we can find.

January 14.- Accompanied by Dr. Jameson and Mr. Nelson we went to Juradó to try to talk with some residents about the possible route through the Paracuchichi to the Atrato and to obtain pawns for the trip. Our absence lasted two days and we observed the two mouths, the curves and other details of the river. The mouth of the Juradó was previously reported as a possible terminal of the canal.

Given the importance of waiting several days to get the necessary pawns in Juradó, I put all the confidence in the person in charge of getting them and deciding for us, waiting patiently until they informed us to be ready to leave.

January 21.- We left the Paracuchichi ranch at ten in the morning accompanied by Dr. Jameson and Mr. Nelson with our guide, and with the laborers, to paddle the two canoes and carry the luggage. I left Captain Rude in Paracuchichi with orders to continue the barometric observations at certain intervals and to monitor the rest of the heaviest and most valuable luggage, including money and provisions with which he should follow us as soon as we informed him of the possibility of crossing the Atrato by this route .

Two of the most trusted pawns were responsible for carrying the surveying instruments. Crossing the estuary in the SE direction we headed towards the mouth of a stream that flows about a mile from the estuary Paracuchichi. We found the mouth clogged by a sandbar; later we assumed that the slower current follows a tortuous path of about 20 yards (18 m) wide enclosed by mangrove forests that generally cover spaces near the coast. We found a few fallen trees that slowed our trip. On each side of the ravine there were easy to dig floods.

The highest tides reach up to two miles (3 km) from the mouth of the estuary. The banks are alluvial but there are no mangroves. There are large spaces covered with bananas, the fruit on which the natives depend, which grows profusely.

From this point the river becomes less deep with the bottom covered with sand and pebbles made of clay. In this part there are six rapids that oscillate between 6 and 18 inches (15 to 45 cm) in height and it is estimated that in total they are about six feet (1.80 m) tall. A mile and a half (2 km) past the tide, we found the mouth of a tributary named Pié de Nequa. There, about 50 yards (45 m) from the mouth, we stopped at three in the afternoon to spend the night and build Ranch # 1.

It had started to rain and continued all afternoon and night causing an increase of several inches in the current. The general direction of Paracuchichi to Ranch # 1 is Northeast.

January 22.- Ranch # 1 is located on a tongue of land formed by a curve of the Pié de Nequa. I measured the height of the river at opposite points, up and down, and found a difference of 2 feet 6 inches (80 cm). The speed of the stream is 18 yards (16 m) for 14 seconds in a small fast and 4 yards (3.5 m) for 14 seconds in a quiet water site.

The shores of land were between 10 and 20 feet (6 to 9 m) above the river level and were made of clay. Only at one point do we find rock that did not protrude from the water. The depth of the water was about one foot (30 cm), so that it could be easily forded. Two other measures of the flow of the current gave 9 yards (8 m) / 14 seconds and 4 yards (3 m) / 14 seconds. The distance measured from this part of our route was 1,000 yards (915 m). We had reached the confluence of a small tributary of the Pié de Nequa in a place called by the natives "Dos Bocas" (Two Mouths).

Here we left the mouth of Pié de Nequa and followed the crest of a hill surrounded by two rivers and continued in a NE direction. The ascent of the hill was gradual with occasional depressions and on each side, separated only by a span. There were ravines 20 to 30 feet (6 to 9 m) deep. The temperature was 84° F at 11 am. We were at 138 yards (125 m) from Dos Bocas.

The crest descended from this point and fell into a ravine that crossed our path and marked the end of a series of elongated hills, of moderate height, composed of clay, which extend in a NE direction a few miles from the Pacific to the Nequa Valley.

After crossing the creek that flowed into the valley, at the right of our route, we climbed an elongated hill in the form of a bale of hay, much lower than the previous ones. We follow it in heavy rain towards the NE, to a place where we decided to spend the night.

The place is located at the mouth of the Chupipi River and is designated in the field manual as Ranch # 2. (See plate where the interrupted line shows the crest and where the level line was drawn and the end of the perpendicular line of points that shows the bottom of said valley).

The distance measured between these two bases was 1,830 yards (1.5 km) to the creek and 960 yards (870 m) from there to Chupipi. At 1 pm the barometer marked 29 20-100 and the thermometer 79° F.

The Chupipi crosses the canal line, flows from the North and continues to the Southwest to join the Paracuchichi. Its small size does not prevent the construction of the canal, but it will be a valuable tributary. The average width is 20 feet (6 m) with an average depth of no more than 2 feet (60 cm). The bottom is of pebbles and there are stratified clay rocks, leaning 20° towards the NE. The riverbanks are high above the water level and are densely populated with trees 60 to 70 feet (18 to 20 m) high.

The marginal spaces of alluvial soil are frequently found in the rivers of the country and are more important for the population as it requires many workers to collect bananas and other food.

January 23.- We stayed at Ranch # 2 waiting for the message from Captain Rude. On the same day, the Chupipi Ranch group started at 7 am. The temperature 80° F. After passing the floor space of the floodplain, the ascent to another hill began in the same way as the others we had previously crossed, preserving the NE direction on the right side of the valley.

At 9 am on the crest of the hill, the barometer marked 28 82/100 and the temperature 79° F. Here the route continued east to the north. The edge was very narrow, and you could hear the waters of the Chupipi at the bottom of the canyon on the left, falling into a waterfall. At 10:45 am there was a heavy storm of lightning and rain of short duration. We continued our journey up and down following the crest until we descended quickly to a ravine where we raised Ranch # 3, two and a half miles (4 km) NE of Ranch # 2. It started raining again very hard all afternoon and night with thunder and lightning. The barometer was at 26 60/100 and the temperature 75° F. The small ravine of Ranch # 3 is only three and a half feet (1 m) wide with high clay banks and muddy bottom. During the rains it takes a lot of water to the canal and can be used as a tributary. The hills and hollows are full of very dense forests.

I must emphasize again, that successively passing over the three clay hills, we have observed a continuous valley of great depth on our right side. Looking carefully to be sure there were no hills that crossed the canal line or other obstacles across the valley, it seems to me that we did not find any.

I also wish to emphasize another important point. Even when we slept every night in the open, protected from the rain under the roof of palm leaves built by our pawns in half an hour, our bed consisted of Indian rubber blankets spread over palm leaves and nobody got sick.

January 25.- We left Ranch # 3 at 9 am and we climbed another hill shaped like a bale of hay formed like the others made of soft clay. In some places the edge was very narrow, it was like the previous ones but less high. Its NE course 12.65 yards (11.5 m) from the Chupador River that crosses the NE.

The Chupador is a tributary of the Paracuchichi. It is 4 feet (1 m) wide, 6 to 8 inches (15 to 20 cm) deep, with clay banks and flows to the SW with little current.

Then we climbed another hill until we reached a gigantic tree compared to the others of medium size but of great height. From there we continued in the same direction and found another creek that reached the Chupador. This was the last trace of water we crossed from the Pacific slope.

We continued ascending through a series of small hills with a plateau at the top. On the left side there was a valley through which the tributary Hingador of the Nequa flows, therefore the first of the Atlantic slope. The Hingador valley is separated from the valley of our right hand that drains the Pacific by the high hill we were crossing. The distance between the two valleys is less than 130 feet (40 m).

Gradually, going down to the NE we crossed two tributaries of the Hingador, and we arrived at a great arm of this river in the union with one of its tributaries that we already mentioned and there we raise the Ranch # 4.

The whole afternoon it rained heavily and continued until midnight. No flooding was observed from the creek. Barometer 28 6/100. This arm of the Hingador is a clear and pleasant creek half a foot (15 cm) deep, 6 feet (1.8 m) wide, a bed of pebbles that flows westward with moderate current.

I must point out that from the last Ranch we continued to see the valley on the right, but I must indicate that near the Hingador the terrain becomes more intricate and there are several branches that leave the center in different directions. Two form a canyon through which the Hingador descends to the Nerqua by a series of waterfalls, the first of which has a height of 160 feet (49 m), the other seven are on average between 3 and 24 feet (1 and 7 m).

This geological formation requires a curve of the canal line to take it to the Nerqua level. The length of the Hingador canyon from the waterfall to the Nerqua in a straight line is less than one and a half miles (2.5 km). A line parallel to the valley where the canal curve (the right-hand valley mentioned above) is proposed up to the mouth of the Hingador could extend the distance a bit.

January 26.- We leave Ranch # 4 at 9 am, successively cross two curves of the tributary and then the main canal of the Hingador that we find grown and muddy by night rain. A fallen tree across the river served as a bridge to cross the current that was too strong and deep to wade through. The rocky bottom was formed by layers of gray slate. From Ranch # 3 to this junction, the distance is 1,660 yards (1.517 m), but since this is not within the limits of the canal, I will not go into details.

The waterfall is a short distance below the crossing and in favorable conditions of the atmosphere you can easily hear it. From this point, we continue the journey through another elongated hill in the Nerqua valley, the foot is crossed by a small rocky ravine that goes to the river.

The laborers got two small canoes from an indigenous resident of Nerqua and in them we traveled a mile to the owner's house, in whose neighborhood at a point located 2⁄3 of a mile (1.5 km), from the mouth of the Hingador we erected Ranch # 5.
Here it was necessary to wait for the arrival of Captain Rude from Paracuchichi with the rest of the luggage and provisions. From here we continued the trip to the Atrato by the Nerqua and the Truandó. Later we realized that the indigenous canoes were too small to carry the equipment, so it was necessary to build a larger one.

The Nerqua has a variable width with an average of 20 yards (18 m). The fords are numerous and reach the knees; the intermediate lagoons reach six feet (1.80 m). The flow is two miles (3 km) per hour. Water like that of all the rivers we cross is sweet, fresh and healthy. It flows through a wide alluvial valley, finely bordered by very fertile forests, with the ability to be grown to produce food for a large population.
Upon arriving at Nerqua at 11:30 am the barometer marked 29 25/100 and the thermometer 80° F.

January 31.- Captain Rude and Mr. Nelson arrived with the rest of the Paracuchichi luggage making the day in 9 hours, with the laborers carrying the luggage. At night a flood of the river raised the canal 3 and a half feet (1 m) so that the pebble beach in front of our camp was flooded, and before dawn it had already passed.

February 1.- In the company of Dr. Jameson, we examined the mouth of the Hingador that is 700 yards (650 m). One of the two mouths remain dry until there is increasing current, among them there is a triangular space of alluvial land.

February 2.- We sent a native to look for the only inhabitant of the river up or down the Nerqua and he returned without him (Juan Domingo) because he was sick. He also said that he had never seen a white man in the Truandó, above the falls, or he would have known.

February 5.-We cut a tree to make a large canoe and with the help of a native, one of his children and with two laborers they finished it.

February 7 and 8.- These days we explored the Hingador from the waterfall to the Nerqua. Two laps below the tree crossing, the river precipitates vertically, falls on a clay ledge about 15 feet (4.5 m), then collapses at a 45° angle over large and irregular dark or black rocks, strong, hard until when It reaches the bottom of the abyss. The amount of water, in ordinary conditions of the river, is small but when it grows, this waterfall must have an imposing aspect due to its great height.
As I mentioned, the river falls between spurs or loins formed throughout the depth of the canyon, so it is necessary to surround the route, to wade the river and ascend in front of the rocks.
The height of the waterfall on each side of the river ranges between 70 and 300 feet (20 and 90 m) of vertical fall. It is formed by hardened black rocks as indicated above. These rocks have crevices that can be easily excavated.

Only in one place of the canyon was landslide observed: a mass of clay had come off the hill peak on the left side and dragged two or three large trees to the bottom of the stream.

In the lower quarter of the waterfall there are hot springs with temperatures of 110 ° F. Under the hot springs, the valley widens considerably; The course of the river becomes tortuous, forming curves with tongues of land in which the vegetation is lush and dense. Finally, enter the Nerqua river through two mouths, one of which remains dry, except when there are crescents.

February 11.- We measure the Hingador waterfall with a line in the following form: length from the summit to the base 230 feet (70 m), depression angle 45°, the resulting perpendicular is 166 feet (50 m).

February 15.- We entered a stream or river that falls into the Nerqua, a mile and a half below the Hingador and followed it for three hours. The same as the latter, is torn by a deep canyon between two edges. It is almost the same size as the Hingador. Then, we found waterfalls that have numerous rapids.

The distance traveled upstream was a mile and a half. It is impossible to climb these rivers because they are full of natural obstacles. It is faster to go half a mile per hour on foot and they are too shallow to navigate even with a small canoe.

We examined another canyon that opens over the Nerqua near our camp. It gives way to a creek that falls 90 feet (30 m) high in a nearby place.

Our workers reported that the canoe was ready and when closely inspected it seemed of adequate size, lightweight, made of cedar, therefore better for navigating rivers in which the main obstacles are fallen trees.

Alejandro and Domingo arrived from Juradó and Paracuchichi with two young and strong Indians and with two of the residents of Nerqua, we intended to reach the Atrato.

February 16.- At 9:30 am we began the descent to the mouth of the Hingador on the way to the Truandó. The Nerqua, lower than the first, was a bit enlarged as can be seen in the table of obstacles. It presents many interruptions such as shallow steps and fallen trees.

We passed the following tributaries that the river receives on the right side: at 10:30 am the Chupachavi, which we had examined on February 14; At 11:20 am the Pavarandó, which we entered on the left side and has a greater current than that of the Hingador. At 2:15 pm the Turniandó, a stream on the left side.

The riverbanks are alluviums with various degrees of hardened clay, usually very soft, sometimes moderately hard and everywhere drilled by land crabs. Some layers of leaves were observed between thick sheets of clay. Also, numerous deposits of blue clay, used by the natives for goldsmithing.

The general course of the river is NE. We arrived at the ranch at 4 pm. The weather that had been magnificent in the morning changed and it started to rain in the afternoon. The barometer indicated 29 2/10, and the temperature 79° F.

February 17.- Starting at Ranch # 6 at 6:45 am, heavy rains at night increased the flow of the river one foot, but it had already descended in the morning. The riverbed is formed by rocky clay slabs. At 7:10 am the barometer was 29 27/100 and the temperature was 75° F. There are only a few obstacles in this part of the river, the current is slow and regular over long stretches, the depth is 4 feet (1 m). At 7:20 am we crossed the mouth of the O'Odor or Oodor on the right bank of a quarter-sized canal that enters the Northwest.

At 8:30 am we arrived at the confluence of the Nerqua with the Truandó, the address of the first East by North. Barometer 29 3/10, temperature 85° F. While we waited, the barometer rose to 29 34/100.

At the confluence we found that it is 5 feet (1.5m) deep and 35 yards (32 m) wide; it flows between alluvial banks, banks that rise 8 feet (2.5m) above the river and are covered with vegetation everywhere. It seems a third larger than the Nerqua in the lowest part of its course. As in this river, the banks are isolated, inhabited only by a native and his family. It flows slowly, 60 feet (18 m) for 35 seconds. The bed consists of fragments of clay rolls.

Associated deposits like those of the Nerqua course, with the same proportion of quartz pebbles or clay stones with quartz veins.

We left the confluence of Nerqua and Truandó at 8:45 a.m. and 10:20 a.m., after crossing some smooth paths of the river with about five or six feet deep, bottom of stratified rock tiles inclined at acute angles, we arrived at the first of a series of jumps or rapids that constitute the greatest difficulty, or danger that we found going down the Truandó.

Our staff spent 5 hours and 20 minutes loading and unloading the luggage in the two canoes through the four rapids. The operation was laborious but necessary to unload the canoes three times and take them overland by the most dangerous places; To lift the canoes especially the biggest one, took great effort and care since were needed to prevent it from crashing against the rocks.

The valley through which this river runs is very narrow, and, on both sides, there are precipices of non-stratified rocks.

At the foot of the fourth jump we raised Ranch # 7 on a rock near the river and high enough to prevent it from being flooded by the rising current. The barometer was maintained at 7 pm on 29/22/100 and the temperature at 78° F.

Between the second and third rapids, the river receives a tributary from the right side, small, 4 feet (1.2 m) wide and only one inch (2.5 cm) deep. Barometer at 7:30 pm was 29 25/100, and temperature 78° F.

February 18.- At 8 am we crossed the river in the big canoe just above the fifth rapid and we went down along the rocks of the shore for about half a mile (1 km). On this site, there is a rectangular curve and we reached the main waterfall 26 feet (8 m) high. It was raining heavily, while the staff was engaged in the difficult and dangerous operation of vacating the canoes, loading the equipment overland to the foot of the rapid and then sliding the canoes on planks, work in which all the members of the expedition participated. After the main waterfall, we passed three other rapids in the same way. At 5 pm, we finish the job without losing or damaging any items.

I must record the way this work was done by Alejandro and the natives who received our praises and thanks from the whole group.
The barometer at Ranch # 8 at 6 pm was 29 30/100. I estimated with the level, the height of the waterfall and got 26 feet and four inches (8 m). The same with the barometer. In the main part of the last rapid, the river receives another tributary from the left side.

February 19.- Today I intended to continue down the river, but heavy rains made it grow 4 or 5 feet high (1 to 1.5 m); The canal is very narrow and rocky. Alejandro did not consider it wise to venture even though after the next bend the river was completely calm.

February 20.- Last night the crescent passed, returning the river to its normal depth. Then there was a storm of lightning and thunder and this morning it had grown more than before and with lots of wood floating in the waters. During our stay at this Ranch, the barometer marked 29 25/100 to 29 40/100.

February 21.- The flow had dropped and at 6 am we left Ranch # 8, and, in a few minutes, we crossed the rough part of the canal to enter calm and wide waters where the Truandó flows after the rapids. At 7:20 a.m., I observed on the left bank the stratified clay tile tilted toward the NE at an angle of 40°. From this point, the banks of the river become flat and all alluvial.
At 7:30 am we passed the mouth of the river called Salida. On the opposite side of his mouth is an island. The Salida River enters the Truandó on the left bank and flows to the SE. The Truandó then passes through the alluvial plain of the Atrato, its margins are all alluvial and certainly very fertile.
At 7 am we passed an arm called Chuparador that forms an island and at 7:25 am we passed another island. At 11:30 am we arrived at the beginning of the Palisades, a series of islands that have their origin in the accumulation of wood carried by the current of the floods. Branches of the river open and close forming a network in this group of islands that stretches for 4 miles (6.5 km).
When the palisades began, it was necessary to drag the canoes over for several yards wide, but after overcoming these obstacles we did not find any other in our descent by the river except one or two trees that we had to cut with the ax to pass.
At 3:20 pm after cutting the last tree we continued down without other obstructions until nightfall. We stopped to spend the night in the canoes because the banks of the river were flooded. The width of the river is 25 yards (23 m) with dense forests on each side of the riverbed. We saw half a dozen unoccupied ranches built by natives and other people of the Atrato who sometimes travel to the Truandó on hunting or fishing trips to the palisades and sometimes to the rapids. The distance traveled during the day, including the stops, current flow and volume of the water passage are shown in the attached table.

February 22.- We left our Ranch # 9 at 6:10 am and continued the trip down the Truandó passing a succession of smooth and slow water paths. At 7:50 am we entered the first lagoon and we found an open and elongated space of ten miles (16 km) in diameter. The entire lagoon is covered with plants that have roots at the bottom and rise several feet high.

We sailed through this green lagoon of the Truandó that receives several tributaries. The banks of the river are full of trees. About 20 miles (30 km) to the north you can see a mountain chain in the NE and SW direction.

At 9:30 am we passed the first lagoon and entered a forest where the Truandó resumes its course in the jungle.

At 11:45 we passed through the mouth of the Chuparador 20 yards (18 m) wide, which flows on NE and SW directions. At 1:30 pm we enter the second lagoon that is equal to the first in form and configuration. After this lagoon, the Truandó returns to its course.

Due to the rising Atrato, the Truandó in this part of the route has no apparent current, therefore we had to row. Finally, at 5 pm we arrived at the Atrato river. The mouth of the Truandó is about 50 yards (45 m) wide but due to the peculiar aspect of the banks of the Atrato, the visibility is low from the Truandó. It is 27 feet (8 m) deep and the width of the bar is 30 feet (9 m). At 5:45 pm we arrived at a village located 200 yards (183 m) below the mouth of the Riosucio river. The barometer indicated 29 37/100 at 6:45 pm. There is a mile and a half from the mouth of the Truandó to Riosucio.

From here we followed Quibdó, the capital of the Province of Chocó where we arrived on March 10. There we spent a month and four days in business not related to this expedition.

We continued down the Atrato and we arrived at the confluence with the Truandó at 6:30 am on April 18, 1855.

At this point began the part of my recognition that was unfinished: the Atrato river from its confluence with the Truandó to its mouth. At the junction of these two rivers, the depth is 58 feet (18 m) and the width 150 yards (137 m) to the north.

At 7:10 am we arrived at Riosucio, we raised a sail at 10:30 am, which increased our speed to 50 feet (15 m) for 14 seconds for 30 minutes (See tables of the Atrato).

At 11:45 am we passed the Salaqui River called Leonda or Yegenta by the natives. The mouth is shallow but opens in a large river. At 7:50 pm we crossed the mouth of the Chacarita.

April 19.- We passed the Salaqui River on the east side. At 8 am we passed through the first mouth of the river called Chocórita and at 10:08 we entered the Gulf of Darién through the Boca Coquito.

I returned to New York on May 27, 1855 and reviewed my notes, mathematical calculations and designs to conclude that it is possible to build a navigable canal at sea-level, without locks, to join the Atlantic with the Pacific, of size large enough to pass the entire World trade in ships.

The plans to achieve this operation can be seen in the five plates with their respective explanations that I am pleased to include in this report. In relation to the healthiness of the route, I have to draw your attention to my meteorological observations and the fact that neither I nor my colleagues became ill during the trip except for an episode of fever and discomfort that I had in Nerqua, without a doubt due to the exercise and exposure to the elements, but since then until my arrival in New York I have enjoyed excellent health.

In relation to the hitching of workers, the four neighboring provinces can supply enough men to carry out the project, some of which are from the Province of Cartagena, and have already worked on the Panama Railroad.

I suggest that the company be carried out in six divisions:
1. At the mouth of the Atrato river
2. In the Truandó river
3. At Townsend station
4. In the East of the tunnel
5. In the West mouth of the tunnel
6. In the Kelley estuary.

To accommodate the necessary personnel to do the job, accommodations must be built with the abundant palms that exist in this part of the country: palm ranches in the 3rd, 4th, 5th and 6th divisions. Those that are needed in the Truandó and in the 1st division in the Atrato, must be floating accommodations because there are no banks or beaches where to build the ranches.
The lodging must be big enough to accommodate the workers of each division. To the east of the summit are the best places to build workshops, deposits in Turbo, near the mouths of the Atrato and at the Townsend station near the junction of the Atrato with the Truandó. Communication between these two points must be maintained every 12 hours by means of six-foot draft vapors.
West of the summit, I propose the best place for supply stores, etc. Gooding and Emma Josefina stations can supply the 4th and 5th divisions. All the necessary vegetables can be grown on the Pacific coast and in the Nerqua Valley, after growing them for a year. Bananas, which are the main food the natives grow in abundance and corn, rice and to some extent in the vicinity of the route there are tropical fruits and tubers. Cereals can be brought from Peru, Chile or San Francisco. Cattle and pigs from Chiriquí to the Kelley Estuary in three or four days. Consequently, there are enough viands for the Pacific divisions.

Before starting the construction of the canal, a horseshoe path must be made towards the summit to bring fresh supplies that can be taken to the Truandó by the same source as in the mouth of the Atrato, that is, Turbo deposits that can receive provisions from New York via Cartagena.

As I mentioned before, a steam can make the trip from Townsend to Turbo in 20 hours and from Turbo to Cartagena in 16 hours in the current conditions of the country. From my great experience, my predilection for the work of people of color is clear because white men cannot make the same effort.

Before finishing, I am pleased to report that my assistants: Captain Norman Rude, Dr. RG Jameson and Mr. Robert Nelson provided invaluable services. Having completed this report with details of the expedition and in order not to prolong myself and waiting for me to receive the results of an impartial investigation, I have the honor to subscribe to you, your obedient servant, William Kennish, New York, August 7, 1855.

NOTE
I think it is advisable to make two tunnels better than one for the following reasons: the width of the tunnel must be equal to that of the river 200 feet (61m) to prevent an increase in current. A single arc that extends all that distance can be very long to be safe, so it must be two arcs (see Section 1 Plate1).

This division also has the advantage of preventing the collision of two ships that cross and must obey the laws of navigation to preserve the right.
As for the height, they must be wide enough for the passage of warships that do not stumble their tallest mast with the tunnel roof.
Frigates and merchant ships usually only need to lower their tallest mast or loosen the cables that hold them erect. All vapors can pass without difficulty.

I refer to the calculation table to estimate the amount of material that must be removed from the river bed: it can be seen that 2/3 parts are rock that form a solid wall on each side that does not need to be covered with other materials, eliminating the need for a major cut, as the lateral slopes of the river beds have an angle of 30° of the perpendicular and the rock is of primitive or basalt formation, which can be easily detonated and at the same time it is easier to remove rock for adjacent valleys than softer material.

In this region there is enough water for hydraulic equipment to lift the rocks or other materials to the shore. A height of 500 to 600 feet (150 to 180 m) of water at each end of the tunnel allows water to be carried by pipe to the canal so that the machines can perform the required operations.

Signed William Kennish, Chief Engineer, August 7, 1855."

Letter from Robert Nelson to William Kennish.
Panama, April 25, 1855
Mr. William Kennish
Dear Sir:
As I think you have already arrived in New York and may be surprised that you did not receive correspondence from me, I regret to inform you that I have delayed in Juradó longer than I wanted or anticipated. I only arrived here yesterday, which explains the delay.
According to your instructions, when we parted at the Truandó waterfall, after

resting for a few days in Paracuchichi, I continued to the Juradó River to explore it and examine the path of the indigenous people through the mountains towards the Salaquí River that flows to the Atrato. Enclosed are my notes.

February 28,1855.- In Alejandro's house at 7 am: Barometer 29.38, Temperature 76 ° F. The rest of the day: Barometer 29.45, Temperature 81 ° F.

March 1.- Same place
6 am Barometer: 29.46, Temperature 78 ° F.
7 am accompanied by a guide and two indigenous people, we sailed in a small canoe at a mile per hour. The current ranges between two and three knots with NW destination.
At 3 pm we arrived at Dos Bocas where the Juradó converges with another river of the same flow. We stopped to spend the night after eight miles down the river.
Barometer 29.4, Temperature 82° F.
6 pm Barometer 29.41, Temperature 78° F.

March 3.-7 am, Barometer 29.4, Temperature 72° F. We sailed until 3 pm when we reached the Antado river, NE general course, distance 12 miles (19 km) along the river and 7 and a half straight miles (12.5 m). The river has many curves and half the size, with mountains on both sides.
Barometer 29.3, Temperature 82°
6pm Barometer 29.25, Temperature 80° F.

March 4.- 6 am Barometer 29.287, Temperature 75° F. The Antado River is the same size as the Hingador near Nerqua. The bed is full of rocks and stones and it is very small for the canoe, so we continued on foot for a mile 2,425 feet in the East direction until we reached a ravine through which we climbed up to 2,000 feet (600 m) in the North direction and reached the height in the direction of Salaquí. Barometer 29.22, temperature 82° F. Then, we continued climbing a very steep slope for about a mile (0.5 km) to the highest part. Barometer 28.5, temperature 82° F. We travelled along the edge in the NE direction more than three miles (5 km) and then went down to the Mojando river, barometer 26.95, temperature 84° F.
From Mojando to Salaquí 4 and a half miles (7 km) NE the terrain becomes flat with few elevations and it is swampy. In the Salaquí the barometer indicated 28.95, and the temperature 82° F.

March 5.- 6 am Barometer 28.92, temperature 73° F. After bringing a canoe that the Indians had hidden, we started sailing until 10 am when we reached the rapids towards the East in straight line, distance plus or minus 12 miles (19 km). The Salaquí River looks the same as the Truandó, the same depth and runs through a valley as beautiful as the Nerqua. Barometer 29.06, temperature 85° F.
As the canoe was too big to drag along the rapids, we left it at the top and walked or rolled along the river bank for more than 3 miles (5 km) but we didn't find any other rapids or a waterfall as big as the Truandó and they informed me that there were no other rapids.

We reached a point in the river that cannot be crossed without a canoe, so we had to go back to pick it up. Barometer 29.1, temperature 82° F. The mountains on the sides of the river at the level of the rapids have the same appearance and height as those of the Truandó, but because of the inclination that is between 25° and 40° I think they can be cut for the canal.

March 11.- We returned to Alejandro's house. So far, I have given you reports of our exploration and observations of the Salaquí River and I leave it for you to form your opinion. I have no doubts, but you will agree with me that the Nerqua route is shorter and easier. I asked Santiago which was the shortest way, and he replied that there was no such way.
Signed Robert Nelson.

Courses and distances

DESCRIPTION
Proposal for the new river aqueduct from the lagoons of the Atrato River to the Pacific to make a continuous communication with the Atlantic Ocean through which large ships can pass through a current of less than two miles per hour.

The premises of this desideratum are based on the following facts:

1. That the average level of the two Oceans is the same.
NE - N
NE
E, N, E
E - E
12,425 2,000
one
3 1,320 4 2,640 30 3,105 12
3 15

2. That the tide at the mouth of the New River on the Pacific coast varies between 12 feet 6 inches (3.8 m) when it is high and 10 feet 11 inches (3.08m) when it falls.

3. That the waters of the Atlantic at the confluence with the New River are 15 feet (4.5 m) 2/10 above the average of the two oceans.

4. That at the highest junction of the Nuevo river is 9 feet (2.7 m) higher than the Pacific at its highest tide, so the speed of the current will be equal to that of the highest part, while at low tide the speed will be equal to 21 and 4,500 feet (6.4 and 1.3 m) of hydrostatic load.

The length of the Atrato river from the proposed junction to the mouth is 61 miles 665 yards (98 km, 608 m) and that of the Nuevo river is 63 miles 1,016 yards (101 km, 929 m). Therefore, they are almost equal, and therefore the time and energy required to climb the Atrato, is offset by the descent by the Nuevo river and vice versa, which is equivalent to navigating 125 miles (200 km) on a level surface.

The highest part formed by the Atrato and beginnings of the Nuevo river have the same height of the average level of the two oceans. Pacific tides would rise along the Nuevo river to near the junction of high tide and will cause an irregularity of the current whose average will be equal to that of the Atrato 2.5 miles (4 m) per hour. As this Nuevo river is destined to flow constantly to the Pacific without obstruction, so that ships can pass continuously, it may be necessary to establish the source from which enough water can be obtained to maintain the flow.

First, the geographical position of the country must be considered: the mountain ranges of South America are parallel to the Pacific. The origin of the Atrato is in the Baudó range and extends through an alluvial valley between this mountain range and the Western mountain range. The river runs in the NW direction towards the mouth. Over the years it has formed a wide and spacious bed that occupies half the valley between the mountains for 300 miles (482 km). The width of the valley in the region proposed for the union is about 50 miles (80 km). This large area can be said to be covered by water with some islands formed by the currents of several smaller rivers that descend into the great river.

The rivers that flow from the mountain range go in the NW direction, those of the Serranía del Baudó have a NE course and flow into the Atrato River, which in turn turns overflowing the banks forming large and extensive lagoons on each side of its course. It is known and it is an established fact that clouds rarely pass through the mountain range, so they discharge rain in the Atrato Valley. This is the reason why it rains almost permanently, with storms of lightning and thunder, while on the Pacific coast there is little rainfall for 8 months a year. This explains the few rivers of that region of the coast in this sector of the country. (See plate # 6).

Because most of the rain falls to the North of the proposed union and is taken to the Atrato by its fifteen large tributaries, in addition to its numerous streams, and the existence of lagoons and lakes whose extension covers hundreds of acres and maintains a supply of water that does not diminish throughout the year, therefore it is possible to have an overabundance of water.

The most important point that has been established and that needs to be confirmed is that the site selected in the Atrato is the best one that can be chosen for this purpose. In the first place there is no point of union of this river with others that flow to the West, as close to the Pacific water level as the Truandó. The Truandó is only three feet (1m) higher than the line and the Pacific, therefore has the advantage to prevent the Pacific tide from flowing to the Atrato and not so high to increase the flow of the Nuevo river at low tide, in effect, keeping the balance with the first.

If the Pocador River or the Naipipi had been selected, the first at 28 feet (8.5 m) above the tide and the second at 30 feet (9.1 m), the rise and fall of the waters of the 16-foot (4.8m) Cupica Bay, then the Pocador would be at 36 feet (10.9 m) above the water level at low tide and 20 feet (6 m) at high. The Napipí 36 feet (10.9m) above low tide and 22 feet (6.7m) above high tide. A canal made in the vicinity of these rivers would have a current of about 5 miles (8 km) per hour.

The Atrato at the junction with Salaquí is only one foot (30 cm) taller than the high tide of the Pacific but the watershed is 1,063 feet (324 m) high above the Pacific and is 30 miles (48 km) wide from Juradó to the other side of the Saw. I personally toured this line and then my assistant Mr. Robert Nelson finished it. (See Letter from Mr. Nelson).

If any of the rivers at the mouth of the Atrato is selected, without referring to the height and thickness of the mountain range, I can see that the high tides of the Pacific are 23 feet (7 m) higher than those of the Atlantic. On the opposite side of the mouth of the Atrato in the SW direction near the Tuyra river or its tributaries Maria, Balsa, Yarisa, etc., all flow into the Gulf of San Miguel. The tide also rises from 25 to 30 feet (7 to 9 m) in Chipaganá, a village located 8 or 9 miles (12 km) north of the Savannah River and while at the mouth of the Atrato, as already said, the ascent and descent are only two feet. Taking the highest tide of the Pacific, that is, 25 feet (7.5 m) and the Atlantic of two feet (60 cm) , the Pacific tide would flow to the Atlantic with a current equal to the hydrostatic load of 11.5 feet (3.5 m) and at low tide the flow would be from the Atlantic to the Pacific of 11.5 feet (3.5 m). In other words, the Pacific would flow to the Atlantic for six hours and from the Atlantic to the Pacific for another six.

Given that the watershed has never been explored, I have heard extraordinary stories told by the natives of the region. During my three visits to the Gulf of San Miguel and its surroundings, the indigenous people of San Blas communicated with the Arquian territory in a short time. But my opinion on this matter is that all information received from the indigenous people must be taken with great caution: the truth or lie of these statements can only be proven with the investigation of the land.

Here I would like to mention for general information that the so-called Darién port is located on an arm of the sea that passes between Boca Grande and Boca Chica, two small estuaries on the Gulf of San Miguel that pass about 20 miles (32 km) up the Savannah river and in the Tayra until arriving at Yarisa, about 20 or 30 miles (32 a 45 km) and I know when I was aboard the HCM Virago steam of Captain Prevost (the first and only steam that has entered that port), which by the tide action was dragged with two anchors and could only stop cutting almost all ties. There is not a single place in this estuary where it can be anchored safely due to the tide.

William Kennish, Chief Engineer August 7, 1855.

The US government sent Lieutenant Nathaniel Michler to confirm the route in the opposite direction starting from the Atlantic to reach the Pacific and presented this report to the Secretary of War in 1861.

Given the observations by William Kennish of the basalt mountain range called Baudo range, we will discuss ideas about how the basalt can be opened to make way to the interoceanic Canal of Colombia.

How to cut the basalt mountain.

LASER is the English acronym for "Light Amplification for Stimulated Emission of Radiation" or Light Amplification by Stimulation of Radiation Emission. By concentrating the sun's rays through a magnifying glass, a high temperature is produced at the focus site that burns the paper. This is an experiment that has been known since childhood.

I would like to share my experience with the use of Laser in neurosurgery, which has helped me to follow with interest the development of high-power Laser weapons and their use for peaceful purposes with a project in mind: the opening of the mountain range Serranía del Baudó, with a high-energy laser that can cut or vaporize the basalt rocks near the Pacific Ocean that stands as a barrier to reach the Atlantic Ocean through the Truandó and Atrato Rivers.

By 1950, Townes discovered the first practical laser. I had the opportunity to be at the University of New York when Dr. Hubert Rossomoff first used the Ruby Laser in Neurological Surgery. Years later at the European Congress of Neurosurgery in Prague, I saw one of my professors, Sidney Stellar, use the Laser to evaporate a brain tumor.

I returned to Bogotá, Colombia where I obtained a scholarship from the Organization of American States and traveled to Chicago to take the course with Professor Leonard Cerullo in the Department of Neurosurgery at Northwestern University. I went to the University of Florida in Gainesville, where I had been appointed Visiting Professor of Neurosurgery by Professor Albert Rhoton and they allowed me to use the Laser laboratory to make a demonstration video of the surgical technique with the CO_2 Laser.

Upon my return to Bogotá to the Neurological Institute, we were able to acquire two CO_2 Laser equipment manufactured in Israel, by the company Sharplan founded by Uzi Sharon and Isaac Kaplan (1919-2012). One of the beams was assigned to the Operating Room and the other to the institution's research and teaching laboratory.

In 1982 we published the first article of our experience in Neurosurgery with CO_2 Laser in the Journal Neurología en Colombia Vol 6: 9. In 1983 we organized the First Latin American Congress of Laser Surgery and courses in Neurosurgery and Otolaryngology in Cartagena with leading specialists from America, Europe and Japan. At that meeting I was appointed first President of the Latin American Society of Laser Surgery.
In 1984 I had the opportunity to be guest professor at the Laser Neurosurgery course at the University of Cincinnati in Ohio by Professor John M. Tew. Then I traveled to Melbourne, to the Congress of the Australian Society of Neurosurgery, where I gave

several lectures in Congress and in the Department of Neurosurgery at the University of Sydney.

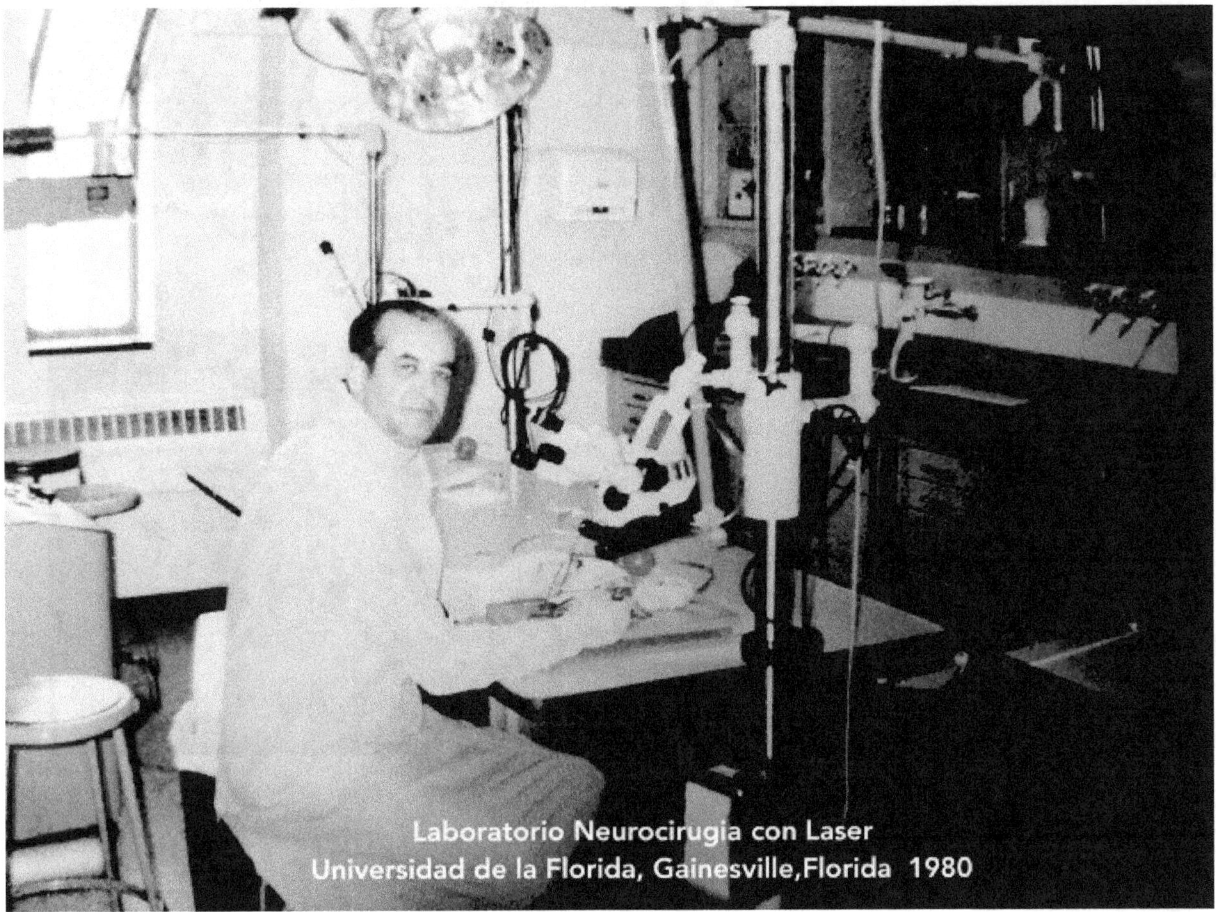

With the possibility of using high-energy Laser equipment that reaches 150 KW, it is much easier to cut the mountain by vaporizing the basalt rocks. It is necessary to know if this High-Power Laser (HEL) equipment can pass through the water to cut the bed of the canal; the reason is that the CO_2 Laser stops with water. The Nd-YAG Laser can be transmitted through optical fibers and can cut underwater.
These high-energy beams have been developed by the armies of the United States and Germany and have been tested as weapons to destroy rockets, tanks, warships, etc. Maybe they can also have use for peace and for the benefit of the world.

6. 19TH AND 20TH CENTURIES:
PANAMA CANAL

In 1849, Colombian President Jose Hilario López signed the contract for the construction of the Panama Railroad with a US company. The 47.8-mile (77 km) line began to be built in 1850 and was completed five years later. The success was immediate by the large number of travelers on the eastern coast of the US who were heading to participate in the California Gold Rush.

In 1876 the President of the United States of Colombia Aquileo Parra Gómez signed with the representative of the Government of France Lucién Napoleón Bonaparte Wyse the treaty for the construction of the Panama Canal by the French company of the Interoceanic Canal. The treaty was approved by the National Congress of Colombia.

The Panama Canal was built between 1870 and 1914. Initially the workers of the French Company had serious health problems due to yellow fever and malaria that caused great mortality. The company failed and was retaken by the United States Government who supported the Independence of Panama from Colombia and built the Canal that celebrated 100 years in 2014.

Fernando de Lesseps, builder of the Suez Canal decided to build the Panama Canal. Through bond issues, the French company began work in Panama in 1870 with the idea of making a canal at sea-level in the narrowest part of the Isthmus. The route extends between Colon and Panama City, for a total of 51 miles (82 km). The camps, two hospitals were prepared, and equipment was imported from France and the United States.

There were three factors that made the company fail: First, the lack of complete engineering studies; second, the use of small wagons to remove millions of tons of dirt and clay from the Culebra cut and third, the epidemics of yellow fever and malaria that caused the death of more than 20,000 workers, including a considerable number of French engineers. The Interoceanic Canal Company declared bankruptcy and organized the New Canal Company, which sold its assets to the United States for forty million dollars (US $ 40 million including the Panama Railroad built by an American company in 1855).

The Government of Colombia denied the approval of a treaty with the United States to make the Canal, in the Department of Panama, citing as matters of national sovereignty. The United States and President Theodore Roosevelt supported the independence of the Department of Panama from Colombia and signed the Hayes-Bruneau-Varilla treaty in 1903.

The Commander of the Colombian troops was deceived in Colon, traveled to Panama City on the Railroad and was separated from his battalion of 1,000 soldiers who returned to Colombia without having fired a single shot.

The success of the Americans was due to the work of General Medical Gorgas, who had met Dr. Finlay in Cuba who had done research on the transmission of yellow fever by Aedes Aegipty mosquito. Dr. Gorgas proceeded to eliminate all the mosquito breeding sites as had already been done in Havana, to provide Panama City and Colón with aqueduct and sewage system. All the receptacles where there was water were covered and all the wells where the mosquitoes had laid their eggs were fumigated. He even changed the holy water of the piles of the churches where mosquito larvae had been found daily.

Regarding the locks, they were designed to raise and lower ships between the Atlantic and Pacific oceans. They created the lakes of Gatún and Miraflores to feed the locks on the slopes of the two oceans.

Finally, the railroad was used to remove the debris from the excavation especially in the sector of the Culebra, where a highly unstable area that causes frequent avalanches was found.

In 1914, ten years after restarting the works, the Panama Canal was opened. Colombia received compensation of US $ 25 million from the United States.

INTEROCEANIC
CANAL STUDIES 1970

SPECIAL REPORT

OF THE

GOVERNOR

OF

THE PANAMA CANAL

ON THE

ATRATO-TRUANDO CANAL ROUTE

UNDER PUBLIC LAW 280
79th CONGRESS, 1st SESSION

THIS SPECIAL REPORT SUPERSEDES ALL REFERENCES
TO THE ATRATO-TRUANDO CANAL ROUTE CONTAINED
IN REPORT OF THE GOVERNOR OF THE PANAMA
CANAL, DATED NOVEMBER 21, 1947, UNDER PUBLIC
LAW 280, 79th CONGRESS, 1st SESSION.

THE PANAMA CANAL AND THE COLOMBIA CANAL

The Panama Canal document (above) shows the laborious process of building the new locks which were started in 2006 when the largest ships were 14,000 TEU. This is a unit that indicates the number of containers that a ship can load. To celebrate the first centenary of operations, the Panama Canal Authority (who manages the Canal), contracted with a consortium of engineering companies the works to make new locks. The work was plagued by setbacks, by strikes of the workers' union and by the demands of the builders to make new contracts for overpricing of the work. New locks were built on the Atlantic and Pacific coasts with 16 gates, designed in Italy and built in South Korea, each gate weighing 4,000 tons.

Ten years later the work was inaugurated at a cost of more than five billion dollars that will be paid in one or two years of operations of the canal. The dilemma is that during this decade the shipbuilders increased their size because the more containers they can load to transport, the value is reduced, so that the current fleet is made of ultra large container ships (ULCS) of more than 18,000 TEUs and the SUEZMAX of 20,000 TEUs are already being built. Therefore, the problem is that the locks are 366 meters long and the ULCS 400 meters of length. All these giants only pass through canals without locks such as the Suez Canal or the future Colombian Canal.

The Colombian Canal was ordered by the laws of Colombia in 1964 and 1984. The first law # 53 of 1964 signed by President Guillermo León Valencia authorized the Minister of Public Works Tomás Castrillón Muñoz to hire Engineering and Economics studies with two New York Companies. In 1984 a new law with the same number, ordered for the second time, the construction of the Atrato Canal. It was signed by President Belisario Betancur. Unfortunately, these laws have not been complied with and this mega infrastructure work continues to be ignored.

Another important and recent news has been the extension of the Suez Canal by the Military Engineers of Egypt. Toll revenues increased to $ 9.5 billion a year.

Meanwhile, Chocó is debated in a humanitarian crisis denounced by the Bishops in 2014, confirmed by the Ombudsman and the United Nations Office for Human Rights. Colombian authorities persist in the oblivion and abandonment of Chocó, a historical situation like that suffered by the Department of Panama when it was part of Colombia.

The Colombian Canal could be built by Colombian Military Engineers with technical assistance from the UNESCO Water Center. It can employ 200,000 workers that can be distributed on ten or twelve work fronts. This is the solution to the 62.8% unemployment of Chocó.

On July 20, 2019 the Chocoanos again entered the civic strike, one of many which have been done before the indifferent gaze of the leadership of the country. The grievance memorial urges to provide health and education services. This cannot be achieved unless the Country has a permanent source of income. The Colombian Canal could be that source of funding. The Atrato, is the fourth largest river in the world, and can be connected to the Pacific Ocean by a 107-mile (172 km) canal, without locks or tunnels. It needs an open pit cut in the lower part of the Baudo range and a railroad to mobilize 100 million tons of rock to lift and protect the banks of the Canal from erosion. It is worth remembering that the Cerrejón coal mines in Colombia produce 32 million tons per year.

This is a very feasible work that can be started with resources obtained from the sale of wood from the Canal area, 492 feet (150 m) on each side of the 107 miles (172 km) long line between Coredó in the Pacific and Unguía in the Atlantic. The Private Association of the owners of the Canal Zone, CANATCOL, AP is committed to reforesting the entire area with Caribbean pines a program like Gaviotas, Vichada, a wonderful work that few know about in Colombia.

7. 20TH CENTURY
EXPEDITION ATRATO-TRUANDÓ CANAL, 1949

I write these lines 70 years after the Colombo-American Commission made the exploration of the Atrato-Truandó Canal Zone, based on US Law 280 of 1949.
It's 264 years since the Atrato-Truandó route was discovered in the fifth expedition sponsored by the Wall Street banker, Frederick M. Kelley in New York.
In 1947 the first Colombo-American expedition with the collaboration of the Engineer Belisario Ruiz Wilches toured the area, made soil and geological studies that served as the basis for the second expedition.

The US engineers, officers of the USACE Army Corps of Engineers, are part of the International Water Management Center: "International Water Resources Management" which could assist in the construction of the Colombian Canal given their previous experience with the construction of the Panama Canal.

There are geological, engineering studies of the route between Humboldt Bay and the Gulf of Urabá following the Atrato-Truandó route. The main obstacle where 85% of the work is estimated is in the cut of the Baudó range, where an open cut of 2.98 miles (4.800 m) long by 492 feet (150 m) wide at the base and 92 feet (28 m) deep is needed.

The most convenient layout is between Coredo in the Pacific (7.06-77.67) and Unguía in the Atlantic (8.05. -77.1), crossing the municipalities of Juradó, Riosucio, Unguía (Chocó) and Turbo (Antioquia). The route must pass east of the Peyé river and the Tumarandó marshes in Turbo territory, to cross east of the Katíos National Park, a natural protected reserve.

The section of the Baudó range is 16 miles (26 km). The journey to Riosucio 34 miles (54 km) and to Unguia 57 miles (92 km) for a total of 107 miles (172 km). The speed of the current is 2 miles (3 km) per hour.

The geology of the area and the branches of the Serranía that extend in the northwest direction, are the only solid part formed by a basalt rock formation. The rest of the Canal Zone is swampy, and alluvial land easy to dredge.

As for the two terminals of the Canal, Unguía is the ideal place to make a deep-water port with a bathymetry of 295 feet (90 m). There ends the Tarena river, one of the branches of the Atrato delta. In Coredó the depth is 33 feet (10 m) which increases to 65 feet (20 m). It needs to be dredged at 92 feet (28 m) for the arrival of the ULCS Ships.

LAWS ON THE CANAL

In 1949 a mixed commission from the US and Colombia, co-directed by Belisario Ruiz Wilches and Julio Fajardo from Colombia, carried out the hydrological studies of the Atrato-Truandó Interoceanic Canal. Major Luis Laverde Goubert also participated as Military Attaché.

In 1964, the Agustín Codazzi Geographic Institute made the topographic survey at a 1: 25,000 scale of the canal route. The plates rest in the archives of that institution. Currently, there are satellite photographs with a definition of 98 feet.
Also, in 1964, Law 53 of Colombia ordered the contracting of Engineering and Economics studies with two New York companies: TAMS and Nathan. The use of nuclear energy to open the Serranía del Baudo was recommended, which was rejected.

In 1970 the US Commission for the Interoceanic Canal was formed. Route # 25 was considered the only one to make a level canal without locks. In the 1970s The Hudson Institute in New York proposed damming the Atrato and San Juan rivers to make two large lakes, generate hydroelectric power and communicate the oceans. The project was rejected due to its ecological implications.

In 1984 the Colombian Congress passed Law 53 ordering the construction of the canal, with the limitations indicated. The author of the Law was Senator from Chocó, Daniel Palacios Martínez. One of the stipulations is that "only national entities or shareholders could be members, foreign persons or legal entities cannot be partners."

In 1996 the President of the Geographical Society of Colombia Alberto Mendoza Morales published the book "El Canal Atrato-Truandó", a committee was created for the construction of the Canal, a forum approved the project, but it was never carried out.

Three hundred publications have been made on the Interoceanic Canal of Colombia. In the library of the Superior School of War, 19 theses were carried out by high-level military officers on the Canal. On one occasion it was estimated that the cost of the

Canal was higher than Colombia's national budget and the opportunity to have a feasible project was ruled out.

Thirty-five years later there is no regulatory decree of the law. According to Senator Palacios Martínez, the law is in force because there is no other that annuls it. According to the Government of Colombia, the law expired, since it was only valid for four years.

In contrast, the Nicaraguan Government of Daniel Ortega passed the 800 Law in July 2012, financed 30 billion dollars for construction with a Chinese firm in September and in January 2013 contracted the Royal Dutch Company to do the project. Income of one billion dollars per year was estimated when the canal started operating, however the company that would finance the canal, declared bankruptcy before starting the works.

The Panama Canal is the source of 70% of that country's GNP. Originally, it had three locks110 feet (33.5 m) wide by 1050 feet (320m) long. Considering the increase in size of ships, Panama decided to build a fourth set of locks for ships 180 feet (55m) wide by 1200 feet (366 m) long, and 60 feet (18 m) deep. The expansion was completed in 2014. When operations began, Ultra Large Container Ships (ULCS) of 1300 feet (396 m) and more feet in length would not fit through the new locks. For this reason, a new Canal is needed for these large ships, which will be 85% of the merchant fleet in year 2030.

Por la cual se autoriza al Gobierno Nacional para elaborar estudios de un Canal Interoceánico.

EL CONGRESO DE COLOMBIA

DECRETA:

ARTICULO PRIMERO.- Autorízase al Gobierno Nacional para elaborar estudios de viabilidad técnica y económica y preparar diseños completos de un Canal Interoceánico por la Hoya del Río Atrato y a través de la Serranía del Baudó.

ARTICULO SEGUNDO.- En los estudios que se adelanten deberá participar personal técnico colombiano.

ARTICULO TERCERO.- Para el cumplimiento de la presente Ley, el Gobierno Nacional podrá contratar empréstitos internos o externos, abrir créditos o hacer los traslados necesarios en los presupuestos de las próximas vigencias.

ARTICULO CUARTO.- Esta Ley regirá desde su sanción.

Dada en Bogotá, D.E., a

Este Proyecto de Ley es presentado por el suscrito Ministro de Obras Públicas.

TOMAS CASTRILLON MUÑOZ

Ministro de Obras Públicas

Law # 53 of 1964

Engineer Tomas Castrillón Muñoz, illustrious and former Governor of Cauca, was Minister of Public Works of the Government of President Guillermo León Valencia. He wrote an essay on the Atrato Canal in the Javeriana Magazine in 1964 and made an excellent summary of the history of this waterway. It could have been the statement of reasons for the law # 53 approved by the National Congress and ratified by President Valencia.

The Engineer Castrillón Muñoz recalls some information on the chronology of ideas on this route, which has been treated since the time of Vasco Núñez de Balboa.
The Minister says "In 1851 Congress approved two contracts with Drs. Manuel Cárdenas and Florentino González to build a canal to put the Atrato river in communication with the Pacific Ocean. In 1852 the Trautwine Engineer sponsored by Frederick M. Kelley studied three routes. In 1858 General [sic] Michler studied the Atrato-Truandó route to go to the Bay of Colombia. "

In 1855 the Law of April 28 contracted with José Gooding and Ricardo Vanegas, the construction of the Interoceanic Canal.

In 1866 the General Tomás Cipriano de Mosquera, in a letter from the General's own hand, to Mr. Eustacio de la Torre contracted the construction of the Canal, approved by Law of June 27. In 1870, the US Government sent Commander Selfridge and Lieutenant Collins to study the Napipí River route.

Humboldt quoted that "following a dispute between the Mosquera and Salinas families, the dispute was resolved with the opening of a trench, where the Mosquera's commissioned the Priest of Novita Fray Pedro Cerezo or Fray Gabriel Arrachategui, to execute the work and unite the two oceans. "

Kennish proposed in 1855 to cross the Baudo range with two tunnels 2.8 miles long, with two work fronts, which could be done by coal miners. Michler in 1858 confirmed the Kennish route and agreed with the excavation of the tunnels. His report was presented to the US Congress in 1861. Frederick M. Kelley proposed to President Buchanan, Queen Victoria and Napoleon III the construction of the Canal, but the Civil War of the United States interfered with the construction of this project. The studies were forgotten, only Father Jesús Emilio Ramírez, SJ remembers them in his article, so it is presumed that these books should be in a library of the Jesuits in Colombia.

According to Castrillón Muñoz, cutting the Serranía by conventional procedures would mean removing 887 million cubic meters of basalt. In Michler's estimate (1861), the total, including the two 2.8-mile-long tunnels, would be 54,781.300 cubic yards.

Engineer Castrillón Muñoz was possibly the first to recommend explosions of nuclear energy to open the Baudo range. This was repeated by the investigations of the US Commission for the Interoceanic Canal published in 1970 in seven volumes, of which the V corresponds to the route # 25, the only one of 30 routes where a canal can be made at sea-level. Alberto Mendoza Morales et al. in his book on the Atrato Canal in 1996, also refers to the use of nuclear explosions to cut the Serranía del Baudó.

It is curious that the Commission's publication does not refer to alternate route # 25A mentioned by Lindner of the United States Army Corps of Engineers in 1969. He says:

"the alternate route begins 8.9 miles north of Riosucio and is directed straight to Colombia Bay." In our humble opinion it is the best route of all, the shortest, easiest to dig and ends near the new Puerto Antioquia that is being built in Bahía Colombia, Municipality of Turbo, Department of Antioquia.

Senator Daniel Palacios Martínez, was the author of Law 53 of 1984. I had the honor of receiving his visit at my residence in Jupiter, Florida, on December 27, 2012, with the gift of the book by Alberto Mendoza Morales et al: Canal Atrato-Truandó, Geographic Colombian Society, Bogotá 1996. The dedication reads: "For Dr. Jaime Gómez, MD interested in the Chocó and Colombia program."

Senator Palacios died in Bogotá on December 26, 2016. Before he died, he phoned me from Bogotá to tell me that "Law 53/1984 had not expired because there had been no other law that had repealed it."

EL CANAL
ATRATO-TRUANDÓ
ALBERTO MENDOZA MORALES
REALIZACIÓN
Dora María García
María Fernanda García
SOCIEDAD GEOGRÁFICA DE COLOMBIA
BOGOTÁ DEL MUNDO

DECREE - LAW No. 53 OF 1964

Law 53 of 1964 by which the National Government is authorized to elaborate statutes for an Interoceanic Canal.

THE CONGRESS OF COLOMBIA DECREES:

ARTICLE ONE. - Authorize the National Government to prepare technical, feasibility and economical studies and prepare complete designs of the Interoceanic Canal through the hoya of the Atrato river and through the Serranía del Baudó.

ARTICLE TWO. - Colombian technicians must participate in the advanced studies.

ARTICLE THREE. - In order to comply with this law, the National Government may hire small businesses, open credits or seek the necessary transfers of the budgets for the next period.

ARTICLE FOUR. - This law shall govern from its sanction.

Given in Bogotá, Colombia. This Bill is presented by the undersigned
Minister of Public Works
Fernando Tomás Castrillón Muñoz, 1964.

LAW 53 OF 1884

LEY 53 DE 1984
(Diciembre 28, 1984)
Diario Oficial No. 36.831 de 15 de Enero de 1985

Por la cual se ordena la construcción del canal interoceánico Atrato-Truandó y se reviste al Presidente de la República de precisas facultades extraordinarias

EL CONGRESO DE COLOMBIA, DECRETA:

ARTICULO 1o. Ordenase la construcción del canal interoceánico Atrato-Truandó por el Departamento del Chocó.

In 1984, Law 53 ordered the construction of the Colombian Canal. The departments of Chocó and Antioquia, Municipalities of Juradó, Riosucio, Unguía and Turbo have the Canal Zone. The owners of the Canal Zone are the Community Councils and Indigenous Councils (Law 70/1993) who are the owners of fine wood trees evaluated at US $ 3.5 billion (Sanín, 2003) with which the Canal construction can be started.

It is necessary that the Congress representatives of Antioquia and Chocó issue a new law to replace the 53/84 and order the 27 battalions of Military Engineers to make the Canal. Another option is to give the project in concession to a foreign company for 30 years. The Canal will produce US $ 6,000 million dollars a year.

www.sogeocol.edu.co/documentos/elcan_atrato.pdf
[Courtesy of Engineer Jesús Pabón Núñez, Ministry of Transportation and Infrastructure, 2013]

In 1996, by Decrees 0927 and 1017, the Minister of Transportation was ordered to submit a report to the Interoceanic Canal Commission. That report is also not found in the Archives of the Nariño Palace, the Ministry of Transportation or the Planning Department.

The Agustín Codazzi Geographic Institute developed the Topographic Map at a scale of 1: 25,000 Atrato-Truandó, IGAC 1964, based on aerial photographs and topographic surveys. It consists of 28 plates which need to be completed with other plates that must exist of the alternative route # 25A between Riosucio (Chocó) and Bahía Colombia in the Gulf of Urabá (Antioquia).

Letter sent to Dean Diago Franco.

d-civil@unicauca.edu.co
Mr. Dean
Julio César Diago Franco
School of Civil Engineering. University of Cauca.
Popayán, Cauca. Colombia

Dean Mr. Diago Franco,

In 1964 President Guillermo León Valencia appointed Engineer Tomás Castrillón Muñoz as Minister of Public Works. He was the author of an article on "El Atrato Canal", Javeriana Magazine Vol. 61 No. 305 (June 1964), p. 438-450.

Engineer Castrillón Muñoz discussed the history of the Interoceanic Canal and presented to the Colombian Congress the bill that was passed in 1964. The Minister contracted with the Tippets-Abbett- McCarty-Stratton Company in New York to study the Canal. As I was informed by the Ministry of Transportation, these documents were not found in the Archive of the old Ministry of Public Works in Fontibón. This law and another of 1984 expired.

In 1996, by Decree 0927 and 1017, the Minister of Transportation was ordered to submit a report to the Interoceanic Canal Commission. That report is also not found in the Archives of the Nariño Palace, the Ministry of Transportation or the Planning Department.

The reason for this letter is to ask if there is any information in the archives of the Cauca University, or in those of President Valencia or Castrillón. Secondly, if students of the Faculty would accept the challenge to design the preliminary draft of the Interoceanic Canal. The best route is alternative # 25A between Bahía de Humboldt and Puerto Antioquia in Bahía Colombia.

Thanking your attention, respectfully,

Jaime G. Gómez, MD.

LAW OF THE REPUBLIC OF COLOMBIA NO. 70 OF 1993

Whereby the provisional article of the 1991 Constitution of Colombia is developed, and grants ownership of the lands inhabited by Afro-Colombians in the Department of Chocó to the Community Councils of that political division.

LEY 70 DE 1993 (Agosto 27)

"Por la cual se desarrolla el artículo transitorio 55 de la Constitución
Política.

El Congreso de Colombia",

Ver el Decreto Nacional 2941 de 2009

DECRETA: CAPITULOI Objeto y definiciones.

ARTICULO 1. La presente ley tiene por objeto reconocer alas
comunidades negras que han venido ocupando tierras baldías en las
zonas rurales ribereñas de los ríos de la Cuenca del Pacífico, de acuerdo
con sus prácticas tradicionales de producción, el derecho a la propiedad
colectiva, de conformidad con lo dispuesto en los artículos siguientes. Así
mismo tiene como propósito establecer mecanismos para la protección
de la identidad cultural y de los derechos de las comunidades negras de
Colombia como grupo étnico, y el fomento de su desarrollo económico y
social, con el fin de garantizar que estas comunidades obtengan
condiciones reales de igualdad de oportunidades frente al resto de la
sociedad colombiana.

De acuerdo con lo previsto en el Parágrafo 1o. del artículo transitorio 55
de la Constitución Política, esta ley se aplicará también en las zonas
baldías, rurales y ribereñas que han venido siendo ocupadas por
comunidades negras que tengan prácticas tradicionales de producción
en otras zonas del país y cumplan con los requisitos establecidos en esta
ley.

8.0 21ST CENTURY

8.1 PETITION TO THE PRESIDENT OF COLOMBIA

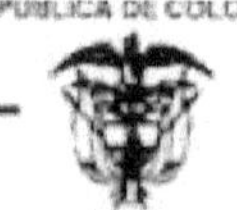

PRESIDENCIA DE LA REPÚBLICA

DECRETO NÚMERO 749   DE 2018

−2 MAY 2018

Por el cual se crea la Comisión Intersectorial para el Departamento del Chocó

EL PRESIDENTE DE LA REPÚBLICA DE COLOMBIA

QUIBDÓ, MAY 9, 2018

FROM:
ATTORNEY
JUAN ANDRES MORENO
SECRETARY CANATCOL AP.

TO:
PRESIDENT OF COLOMBIA
JUAN MANUEL SANTOS CALDERON
PALACIO DE NARIÑO- BOGOTA D.C.

MINISTER OF INTERIOR

MEMBERS OF THE CHOCO INTERSECTORAL COMMITTEE

Bogota D.C., Colombia

REF: RIGHT OF PETITION

Mr. President of Colombia, Minister of Interior and Gentlemen Members of the Chocó Intersectoral Committee,

The owners of the lands of the Chocó Interoceanic Canal zone: Community Councils, Indigenous Reserves and other legal persons of Chocó, within the framework of Law

70 of 1993, we organized ourselves in the entity that is called, PRIVATE ASSOCIATION Canal Interoceánico de Colombia, CANATCOL AP, with Nit. N.900931385-1, all in accordance with Law 1508 of 2012, with the main objective of building the Interoceanic Canal of Chocó, to alleviate the humanitarian crisis in which the Department of Chocó lives and has lived. Humanitarian crisis, in the economic, social, political and administrative, which was denounced by the Catholic Church, the Ombudsman and the United Nations.

As Mr. President is aware that his office, in compliance with several judgments of the high courts, produced Decree 749 of May 2, 2018, creating the INTERSECTORAL COMMISSION FOR THE DEPARTMENT OF CHOCO, in order to deal with the humanitarian crisis in which the Department of Chocó lives and has lived, in the most respectful way we ask you, Mr. President, among the works to be taken into account, as great solutions, it is possible to order the inclusion of the Chocó Interoceanic Canal, whether as a work to perform in the short or long term, as a work of the highest importance, a priority, to solve the humanitarian crisis of Chocó and promote the development of the region and of all Colombia.

We make this request, Mr. President, because if the Interoceanic Canal of Chocó is included in the plans of the Colombian nation, in the short or long term as it should be, everything is more favorable for legal entities that somehow promote that purpose of Homeland. For our organization it is of the greatest importance, to know that it is also a purpose of the Colombian State, to build the Interoceanic Canal of Chocó.

Mr. President, we do not understand the reasons for the government of Colombia, to continue postponing a work of such importance as the construction of the Chocó Interoceanic Canal, a work that will generate foreign exchange, labor and employment to more than one million people between direct and indirect and it is the work par excellence that comes to claim Chocó and implement a development of great importance for Colombia, because the 172 km (107 miles) long canal area, both margins, will necessarily become a pole of agricultural, livestock, industrial and commercial development, for Chocó, Colombia and the world. The construction of this work should be a post-conflict flag.

Mr. President, considering that based on Law 53 of 1964, the plans and economic studies of the Interoceanic Canal of Chocó were contracted with two New York companies. That Law 53 of 1984 ordered the construction of the Chocó Canal. That Decree 0625 of 1996 contracted with the same company of economists in New York an economic study that concluded that the capacity of the new locks in should be expected. That the new 366 m long locks of the Panama Canal, do not allow the passage of ships of more than 400 m in length, that Ultra Large Ships (ULCS) will be 85% of the World Merchant Fleet in 2030, we very resolutely request:

1. That the Universities, National of Colombia and Technology of Chocó be requested to carry out feasibility studies within a minimum period of 12 months including:

A. The modification of the plans elaborated in 1945, 1964, 1969 to adapt them to the ULCS and construction manual in detail.
B. Economic and financial studies in detail.
C. Environmental Studies in detail with route mapping and tree census between Coredó and Riosucio.
D. Detailed audit plan.
E. Obtain construction, environmental, licenses from ANLA to begin construction of the Canal.
F. Plans for the San Pablo Canton Medical Center, where the National University of Colombia will establish a 10-hectare field site donated by the Moreno Lozano family.

The Private Interoceanic Canal Association of Colombia, CANATCOL, AP will pay universities an equivalent of ten million dollars (USD $ 10,000,000) when the canal begins operations, or with the sale of trees that will need to be cut down in the area of the Canal. This amount will be dedicated to the construction of the Faculty of Medical Science and a Level III Hospital of the Canton of San Pablo.

CANATCOL, AP undertakes to reforestation of the same number of trees cut down in Chocó.

Waiting for your approval, we await your response.

Best regards.
Juan Andrés Moreno,
Executive Secretary CANATCOL, AP

8.0 21ST CENTURY

8.2 CANATCOL, AP is the Private Association of Community Councils and Indigenous Reserves, owners of the Interoceanic Canal Zone of Colombia, (Law 70 of 1993). It was incorporated in Quibdó on November 18, 2015. They were elected as members of the Board of Directors:

President:	Leopoldino Perea Caicedo
Vice President:	Yerlin Moña Polpare
Secretary:	Juan Andrés Moreno
Treasurer:	Nilson Mosquera Sierra
Attorney General I:	Gilberto Panesso Arango
Attorney General 2:	Emigdio Pertuz Buendia
Member 1:	Baltazar Mecha Outsiders
Vocal 2:	Oscar Murillo
Member 3:	Francisco Murillo Ibarguen

The main purpose and highest priority of CANATCOL, AP is the construction of the Interoceanic Canal of Colombia.

8.0 21ST CENTURY

8.3 INTERNAL NAVIGATION

Inland navigation along its rivers and canals has been known since ancient times. In Babylon and Egypt, they sailed from the Mediterranean to the Red Sea 15,000 years ago, long before building the Suez Canal.

The longest Grand Canal in the world is in China it is 1776 km (1103 miles) long, and it was built in 605 AD.

Channels run through Europe for hundreds of years. The Erie Canal in the United States was built between 1817 and 1825, is 584 km (363 miles) long, it has 54 locks and was built when there were no Civil Engineers. It communicates Lake Erie with the Hudson River and increased trade and development throughout the Western United States.

The main reason for building canals is that inland water navigation is much cheaper than any other means of transportation.

In the New Granada (Actual Colombia) the Canal del Dique was built around 1650 by the Governor of Cartagena Don Pedro Zapata de Mendoza, connecting the Bay of Cartagena with the Magdalena River.

As mentioned earlier, the first Interoceanic Canal in Colombia was excavated by the parish priest of Novita Gabriel Arrachategui in 1778, linking the Atrato and San Juan rivers along the Raspadura ravine, it is only two meters wide.

The Interoceanic Canal of Colombia is the work that the country is waiting to unite the two oceans through the Isthmus of Darién between Coredó and Unguía, municipalities of Juradó, Riosucio, Unguía (Chocó) and Turbo (Antioquia) and is the only one of 30 American sites where the two oceans can be connected at sea-level. The Colombian Government is expected to replace Law 53 of 1984 that ordered the Construction of the Canal.

https://www.blogger.com/blogger.g?blogID=14509987861208204 35#editor/target=post ;postID=2843178350807564355;onPublishedMenu=all posts; onClosed Menu=all posts; postNum=0;src=postname

The US Commission for the Interoceanic Canal, created by a law of that country, studied in detail 30 probable sites of the American continent and concluded that the only place where a canal can be made at sea-level is in Colombia (Route # 25). The report consists of seven volumes, of which the V corresponds to Colombia.

8.0 21ST CENTURY

8.4 EXCAVATION OF THE CANAL

The estimate of the amount of excavation required for a canal at sea-level on the Atrato-Truandó route is based on traced cross sections that were scaled from a 1: 50,000 scale topography to which they were applied pending lateral static slopes of the material found, the number of cross sections per mile varies from one in the areas of marshland uniform to 14 in the region of the mountain range. The total amount of excavations is 3,213,596,000 cubic yards, of which 1,460,876,000 cubic yards are rock. In comparison, the excavation required for the conversion of the Panama Canal at sea-level is 1,069,000,000 cubic yards, including 793,854,000 cubic yards of rock."

US Law 280 estimated 104.60 miles between Humboldt Bay and the Gulf of Urabá and believed the construction would last 20 years at a cost of USD $ 5 billion. It included a river port 20 miles south of Candelaria Bay in the Caribbean and another in the Pacific.

At present, one must think about modifying the Atrato-Truandó path to eliminate eight curves. The design of the Canal at sea-level for ULCS should be as straight as possible: the route between Coredó 6.93 -77.65 and Unguía 8.25-76.98 would only have an obtuse angle curve at the end of the Baudó Range route in the Northeast direction to continue North to Unguía, where a deep water port could be made. The line would pass east of the Peye River and the Tumaradó marshes, eastern boundaries of the Katíos National Park.

The distance between Coredó and Unguía could be 30 kms (18.6 miles) less than the Atrato-Truandó route. The basalt cut of the Baudó Range is facilitated with the use of two high-energy Laser equipment, one megawatt (Patent number: 8220965/2012). This equipment can be mounted on amphibious vehicles with AVA-7A1 tracks. They can cut eight meters of basalt per hour, which would cut the cost and time in half.

To move 1,069,000,000 cubic yards of the basalt of the Baudó Range, a railroad parallel to the canal is required along the eastern side to make the benches on both banks of the Atrato river and prevent periodic flooding. A Hydrail with hydrogen cell engines and side dump wagons should be considered in the basalt floor part that supports the weight of the train. They are approximately 15 miles from Coredó. Further, it will be necessary to dig the ground to use barges to carry the rocks, because in the swampy and alluvial terrain where perforations were made up to 175 feet deep, no rock was found.

Returning to the study, it was anticipated the need to make a tunnel under the Canal for the passage of the Pan American Highway. There are exact calculations of the slopes of the Baudó Range cut which, due to their basaltic nature, can be almost vertical, but the illustrations show 25-inch steps between the surface of the water and the summit.

Kennish (1855) recommended six camps to do the work, this can result in twelve work fronts. In the lower Atrato there will be a need to use river boats to house the staff, due to flooding. A hospital ship is also needed to care for the sick and cooperatives in each camp to care for the workers. The work must be done in 3 shifts of 24 hours, seven days a week, for that you will need electricity. All workers should be vaccinated against yellow fever, sleep under canopies and use medications to prevent malaria. Logically, you must have a permanent health group to fumigate all the water wells and kill mosquito breeding.

The Suez Canal was recently widened by the Military Engineers of Egypt. Revenue increased from USD $ 5.5 billion to USD $ 9.5 billion annually. How could we get the owners of the Atrato-Truandó Canal Zone, Community Councils and Indigenous Councils of the Municipalities of Juradó, Riosucio and Unguía (Chocó) that make up CANATCOL, AP and Turbo (Antioquia) to develop an agreement with the Colombian Army to make the Canal del Colombia? General Yepes thought it very good to request Technical Assistance from the International Water Center of the US Military Engineers (Law 26 of 1959) who participated in the construction of the Panama Canal.

COREDO 6.93 -77.65 to UNGUIA 8.25-76.98
Municipalities of Juradó, Riosucio and Unguía, Department of Chocó, Turbo (Antioquia)

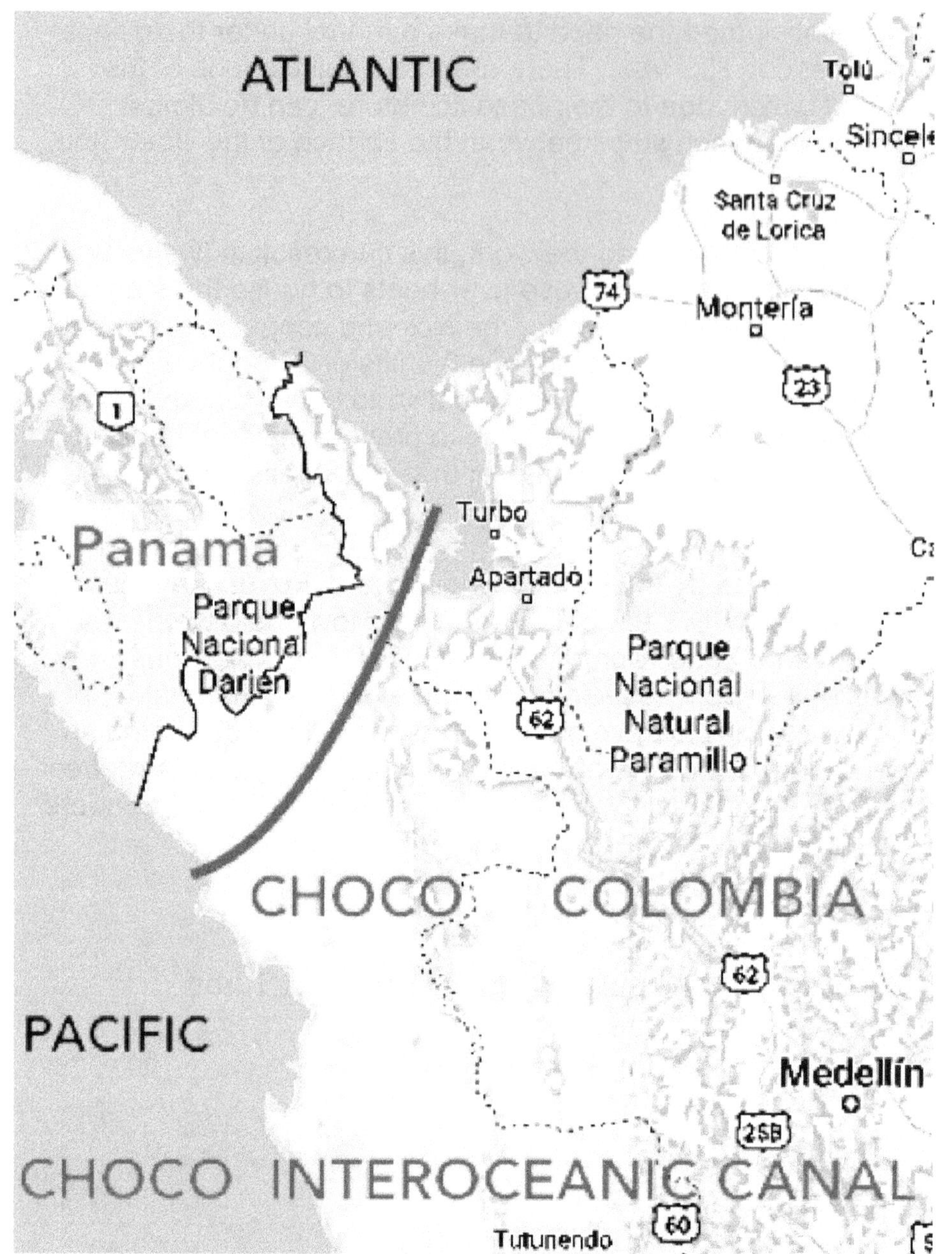

The Canal will begin in Coredó (6.9 3333, -77.65) in the Pacific. The open cut will begin at the intermediate point between the Curiché river lagoon and the source of the Coredó river. The Baudó Range will be reached (3 miles from the beach). It will be crossed through an open cut of 15,748 feet through the basalt mountain (this will be the most difficult part and 85% of the work).

The option of following the course of the Truandó and Atrato rivers proposed in the nineteenth and twentieth centuries is not valid now when the ships are gigantic, difficult to maneuver and make curves. It is suggested to make a route with a single very wide curve.

It is necessary to draw the Canal line to demarcate a 656 feet wide corridor on each side of the line, to make the forest inventory, price it and submit it to an auction. The CN Gustavo Angel Sanín estimated the value of fine wood trees at USD $ 3.5 billion, enough to do all the studies, the six camps and start the work.

Both Kennish (1855) and Michler (1861) proposed to excavate a tunnel 3 miles (4.8 km) long to cross the Baudo Range. Nowadays an open cut is needed in the Baudó Range. Geology shows that the Baudó Range is made up of basalt rock. The slopes were calculated in 1949. The prism must have a base 656 feet wide. The cut is like that of the Corinth Canal that was made in the 19th century when Nobel had not invented Dynamite. The Baudo Range must be cut on both sides at the same time.

There are jumbo machines with pneumatic hammers. After drilling, the perforations can be filled with Expansive Cements [Depandex® or Da-mite®] that fracture the rock without explosions. [Furukawa, and Rodríguez Londoño, FRD, Furukawa SA, Roca Drilling Co. LTD Ave Calle 22 No 34-63 Bogotá, Colombia; Sandvik Hefimec, Ltda. Carrera 62 No. 14 -86, Bogotá].
A better alternative is the use of the High Energy laser: A megawatt can cut 33 feet of basalt per hour; this would reduce time and cost by half.
To flatten the bed of the channel a basalt slicer manufactured by Vermeer model T1655 Commander 3 can be used.
Another possibility is the electric pulse drilling [info @ terracoh- age.com.com j.griffin@terracoh-age.com, John Griffin TerraCOH, Inc. Tel 612-201-6896]

Design.

Given that the new Ultra Large Container Ships (ULCS) of more than 18,000 TEUs are difficult to maneuver, the ideal will be a design with a single radius curve of more than 33,000 feet from Coredó, Municipality of Juradó, Chocó: Latitude: 7.06833 Longitude -77.66537368297577). The cut will begin south of the Curiché lagoon and north of the source of the Coredó river to protect them. It is directed towards the NE; it needs an open cut of 15,748 feet long and 656 feet wide at the base and 92 feet deep.

The line will cross the Baudo Range and will continue directly to a site north of Riosucio to take the line east of the Peyé river and the ceilings of Tumarandó, eastern boundaries of the Katíos National Park and end at the Tarena pipe, Municipality of Unguía. Electric generators will be necessary to allow 24-hour construction in three 8-hour shifts, six days a week, cutting the mountain from both east and west fronts.

To move 100 million tons of basaltic rock (Cerrejón produces 32 M tons of coal per year), a railroad parallel to the canal is needed on the eastern side between Coredó and the end of the foothills of the Baudó Range, (15.5 miles). It would be ideal if it were electric or with hydrogen cell engines, side dump wagons to move the Baudo basaltic rocks and transfer it to barges to take the rocks to the banks of the canal to protect them and make 13 feet tall and wide bases on the eastern side and 3 feet high and wide on the western bank.

Design of a deep-water port in Coredó (Bathymetry shows depths of 33 feet (10 m) to 66 feet (20 m) that must be dredged at 92 feet (28 m) with all facilities).

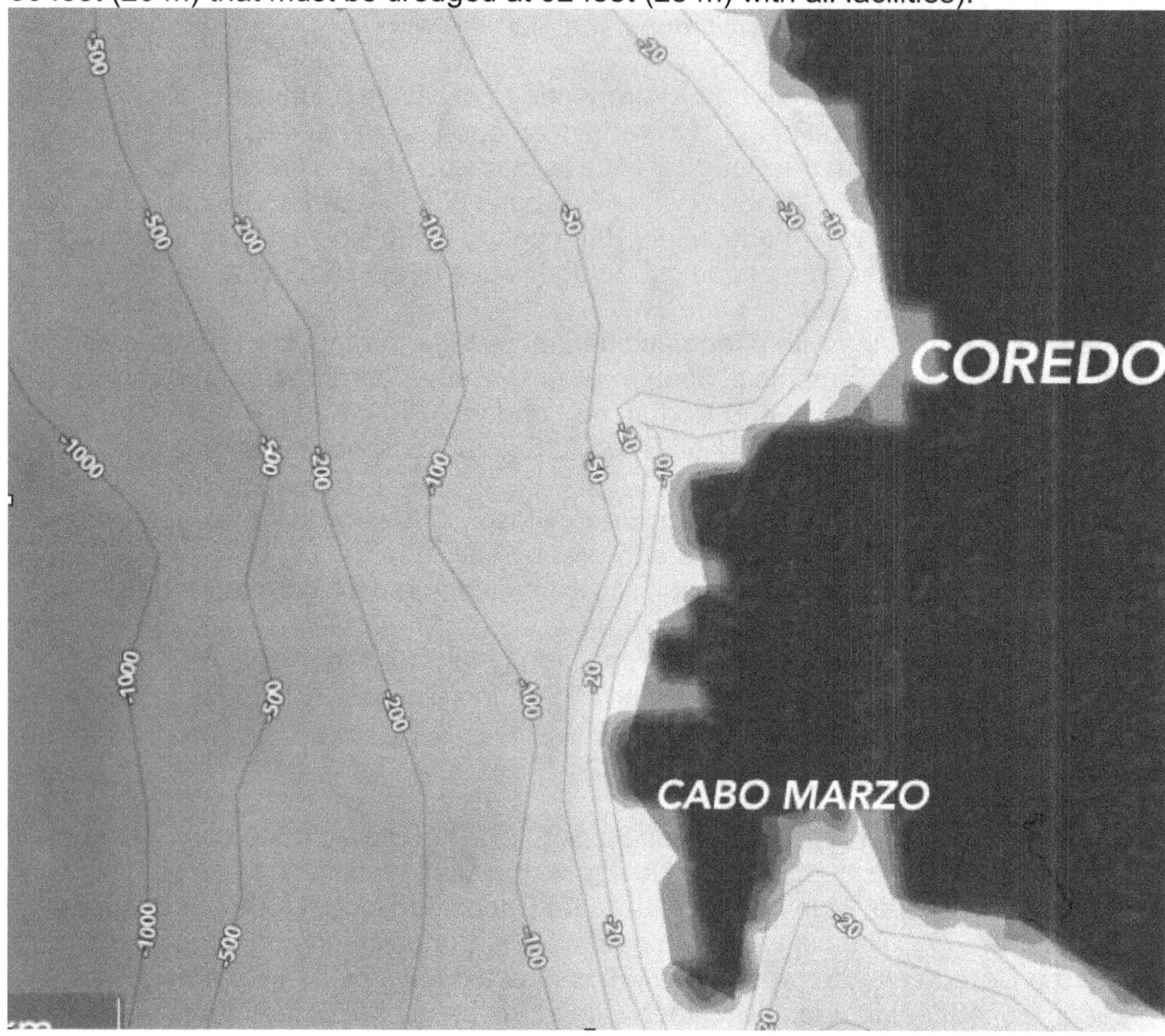

The master plan for the development of a smart city for 100,000 inhabitants, which would eliminate unemployment in Chocó, could include:
• Industrial zone.
• Railway center.
• Heavy machinery factories.
• Shipyard factory.
• International airport in Cabo Marzo.
• 250 MW tidal power plant in the Pacific (13 feet high tides) and another 150 KW geothermal energy at the Juradó, Unguia and Nuqui hot springs, to generate electricity for the Canal Zone.
• Cement plants in Cabo Tiburon and Napipí where there are deposits.

Interoceanic Canal of COLOMBIA
COREDO 6.93 -77.65 to UNGUIA 8.25-76.98
Municipalities of Juradó, Riosucio and Unguía, Department of Chocó, Turbo
(Antioquia) Scale 1: 10.00

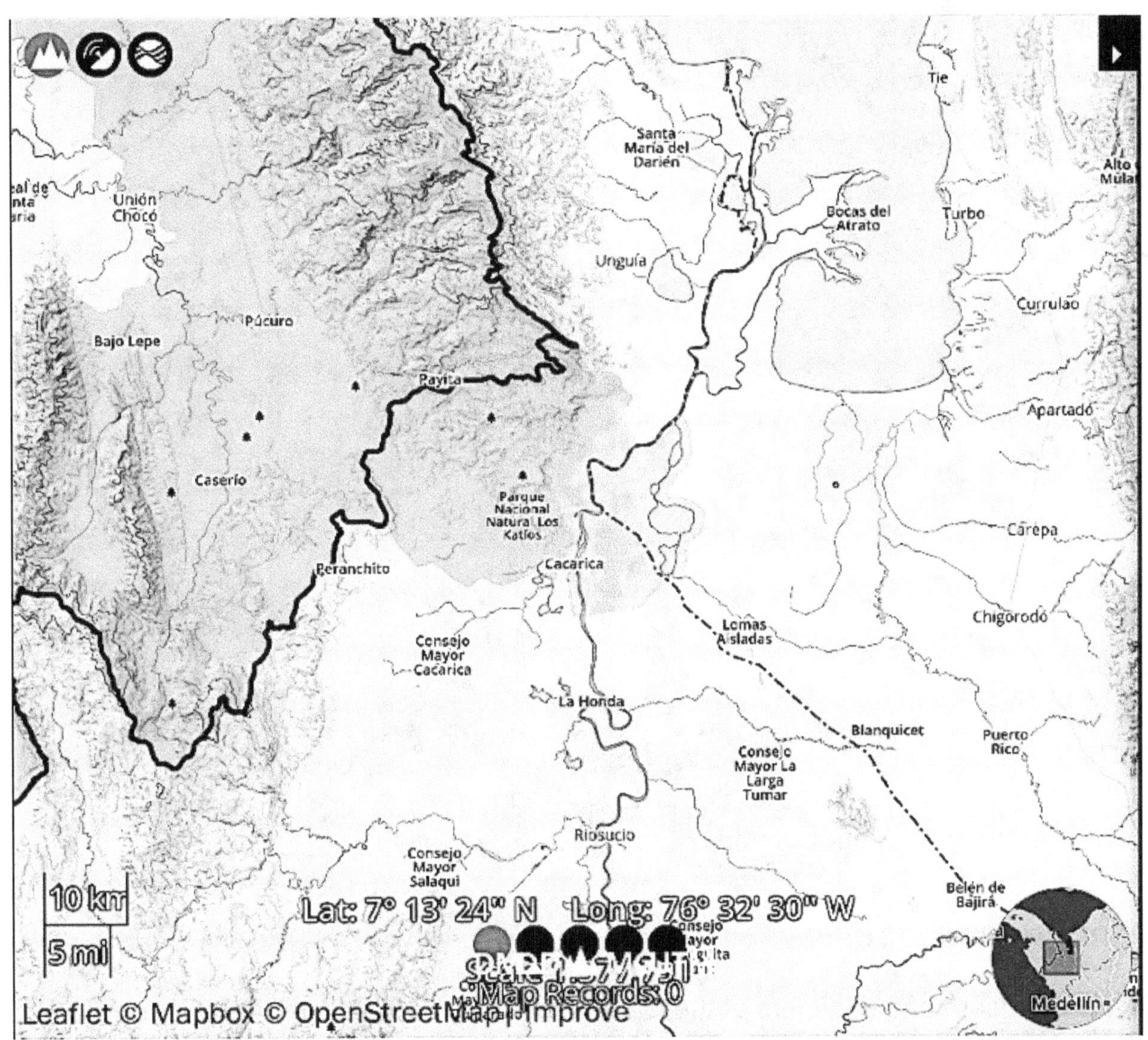

The Interoceanic Canal at sea-level will allow the passage of ultra-large container ships
(ULCS).

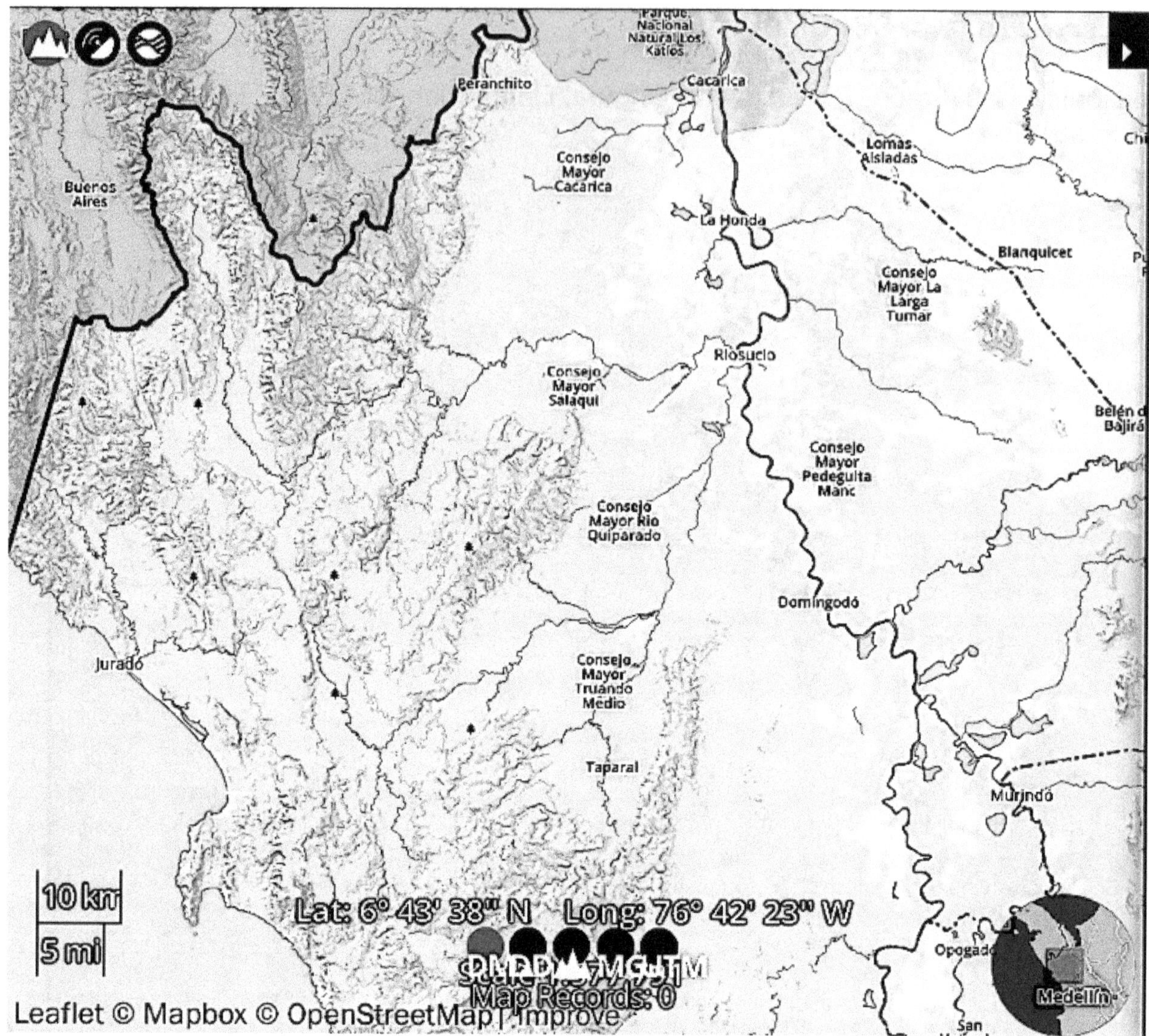

ENVIRONMENTAL STUDIES

The main concern of the owners of the Canal Zone of Colombia integrated in the CANATCOL Private Association is the protection of the environment, mainly because it is their own habitat. The indigenous groups of the Canal Zone consider nature to be sacred, and will not allow CANATCOL to harm it.

The Canal Zone of Colombia is one of the rainiest in the world with places like Lloró where 49 feet of water fall annually. The region is humid, thousands of animal and plant species are found, many of which are still being discovered. The idea of making the Colombian Canal is not to destroy the environment, nor to promote the cutting down of trees, the extinction of these unique species of Colombian fauna and flora or the contamination of water. On the contrary, this project aims at promoting the development of the region, the protection of the environment, through the creation of forest and animal reserves, where the continuation and protection of these species is perpetuated and where it is promoted the procreation and healing of injured animals.

It is necessary to continuously dredge the mouths of the rivers, so that they remain free of sand and thus the ships can navigate. This work with the aquatic element will also include the decontamination of rivers that are polluted with mercury and cyanide due to their use in gold mining. The rivers in the area should be cleaned and promote the breeding of fish and shrimp, which will contribute to the nutrition of the indigenous population in the Canal Zone. Groups of students and clubs (Rotary Club, Lions Club) will be invited to adopt areas of the canal, where volunteers clean the area, remove trash and where methods are used to decontaminate the water.

In order to excavate the Colombian Canal, it is necessary to cut a 62-mile-long zone between Coredó and Riosucio by 948 feet wide. CANATCOL, AP undertakes the task to reforest the area with the same number of trees felled, giving permanent work to Forest Engineers. The Caribbean Pine is a species that has been sown in the Eastern plains of Colombia, covering thousands of hectares and would be a species to be considered for reseeding on the banks of the Colombian Canal.

The Pacific Environmental Research Institute (IIAP) conducted the feasibility study of the Atrato River Navigability sponsored by Invías in 2011. In 2014 the Colombian Society of Engineers (SCI) awarded the Lorenzo Codazzi Prize for this study.
In 1956, the SCI granted the same prize to the prefeasibility study prepared by Colonel Luis Laverde Goubert, a military engineer, who was one of the members of the Colombo-American expedition that traveled the Atrato-Truandó route in the 1940s. The studies determined that the Atrato river is the best navigable waterway in the country. "The methodology of an interdisciplinary working group was used for the biotic, abiotic, socio-economic and cultural characterization of the Atrato navigable channel." The hydro-climatological study of the Atrato River basin and topo-bathymetric survey was carried out with international advice from the Antares Foundation of the Netherlands. The studies concluded that "the Atrato River navigable canal is feasible from a technical, environmental, socio-economic and cultural point of view."

 It is advisable to complete the environmental studies with the same institution of recognized national and international prestige and for this, conversations have begun with the authorities of the IIAP that await the financing of the work to complete the study of the rest of the route of the Canal Zone between UNGUIA 8.0467 ° N, 77.0932 ° W, where the Tarena pipe ends, (one of the branches of the Atrato River delta, where there is the possibility of making a deep water port) and COREDO 6.93333 ° N -77.65 ° W in the Pacific , south of Humboldt Bay and protected by Cape March. The Canal Zone includes the municipalities of Juradó, Riosucio, Unguía (Chocó) and Turbo (Antioquia).

9. 2019 BILL OF LAW

A bill by which the construction of the Interoceanic Canal of Colombia is ordered, and other provisions are issued. The Congress of the Republic of Colombia decrees:

ARTICLE ONE:
Include the Colombian Canal (Unguía-Coredó), Municipalities of Juradó, Riosucio, Unguía (Chocó) and Turbo (Antioquia) within the National Road Plan as a project of global public interest, with maximum priority for its construction, operation and maintenance.

ARTICLE TWO:
Build the Interoceanic Canal of Colombia between Corredó 6.93 -77.65 and Unguía 8.25-76.98.

PARAGRAPH: Recognize the Private Association Canal Atrato-Truandó, Colombia (CANATCOL, AP) established in accordance with law 1508/2012 and integrated by the owners of the Canal Zone: Afro-Colombian Community Councils and Indigenous Town Halls of the Municipalities of Juradó, Riosucio, Unguía (Chocó) and Turbo (Antioquia). (Law 70/1993).

ARTICLE THREE:
The work of the Interoceanic Canal of Colombia will have maximum priority as the most profitable infrastructure work that Colombia can do.

ARTICLE FOUR:
The loans that are necessary for the construction of the Canal will be guaranteed by the State through FINDETER, the National Development Finance Corporation (FDN), and other credit institutions.

ARTICLE FIVE:
Technical assistance will be requested from the Water Center of UNESCO LATIN AMERICA (Law 24/1959).

ARTICLE SIX:
Exemption of all taxes for the construction of the Canal and for a period of ten years is granted to all industries established in the territory of the Canal Zone.

ARTICLE SEVEN:
The export of raw platinum ore is prohibited and the construction of a refinery in the Department of Chocó controlled by the Bank of the Republic is required.

ARTICLE EIGHT:
Impose a 50% tax on the exploitation of the natural resources of the area (Gold and Platinum) of the Atrato-Truandó Canal of Colombia. These resources will be dedicated to the Construction of the Atrato-Truandó Canal, Colombia at sea-level, the

maintenance of said canal and the socio-economic development of the Atrato-Truandó Canal Zone.

ARTICLE NINE:
The destruction of heavy equipment confiscated from illegal miners by the armed forces is prohibited. It is ordered to deliver them to the military engineers to dedicate them to the work.

ARTICLE TEN:
It is ordered to contract with a Faculty of Civil Engineering of a Colombian University the preparation of the pre-feasibility studies, feasibility, environmental studies, construction plans of the Colombian Canal, to deliver it within a year from the date of the contract.

ARTICLE ELEVEN:
This law exceeds any other law, decree or provision that is contrary to it, as it is a public utility project and construction must begin within 45 days after obtaining the corresponding licenses. It will begin with a mission of military engineers and agro-forestry engineers to demarcate the route, take inventory of fine wood to sell it to finance the first stage of the project.

ARTICLE TWELVE:
Modify the National Shield: The third quarter with the Isthmus of Panama will be replaced by the Colombian Canal.

PARAGRAPH: The Ministry of Transportation and Infrastructure is ordered to prepare the regulation of this law within 45 days. This law will govern from its publication in the Official Gazette.

10. BUSINESS PLAN

Colombia Interoceanic Canal, CANATCOL, Private Association

CONTENT
    1. Executive Summary:

        a. Mission
        b. Goals
        c. What has been done?
        d. What is needed?

    2. Department of Chocó
        a. Resources
        b. Communications, Infrastructure

1. Executive Summary
a. Mission

Private Association Colombia Interoceanic Canal, CANATCOL, AP Colombia.

CANATCOL, is a Private Association composed by the owners of the Canal area, Colombia, in the Municipalities of Juradó Riosucio and Unguía (Chocó).

CANATCOL, AP was established under the Law of the Republic of Colombia # 1508 of 2012. The owners of the Canal area are the Afro-descendant Community Councils and the Indigenous Councils of the mentioned municipalities. (Law # 70 of 1993).

CANATCOL, AP was constituted by public deed in November 2015 and registered with the Chamber of Commerce of Quibdó, NIT No. N900 931 385-1.

CANATCOL, AP seeks to end the humanitarian crisis denounced by the Catholic Bishops and confirmed by the Ombudsman's Office and the United Nations.

CANATCOL, AP respects the customs and traditions of the owners, seeks to improve health, nutrition, education, housing and welfare conditions.

The highest priority of CANATCOL, AP is the construction of the Interoceanic Canal to produce a continuous flow of funds that allows the harmonious development of communities.

CANATCOL, AP plans to provide the Department of Chocó and the Municipality of Turbo with the necessary electrical energy for industries, to provide pure water to all inhabitants, to build wastewater treatment plants to prevent damage to nature.

b. Goals

CANATCOL, A.P. proposes to inform all the inhabitants of the departments of Chocó and Antioquia of the need to discover the hidden treasure they have for the benefit of the community.

CANATCOL, AP seeks to create wealth with a continuous flow of dollars to devote to the solution of the humanitarian crisis, health, education and welfare and development of the hidden potential of the areas occupied by their owners.

The highest priority is the construction of the Interoceanic Canal at sea-level between Coredó 6.9 3333, -77.65 and Unguía 8.25, -76.98

c. What has been done?

c1. Prefeasibility Study: Thesis Colonel Luis Laverde Goubert, Superior School of War, 21956. Lorenzo Codazzi Prize. 600 Pages, copies typed in Superior School of War and SCI.

c2. Plans and economic studies of the Atrato-Truandó Canal made by the Governor of the Panama Canal (US Law 280 signed by President Harry S. Truman).

c3. Plans and economic studies of the Atrato-Truandó Canal made in New York by Tippetts-Abbett-McCarthy-Stratton (TAMS). Nathanson, 1965 (LAW 53/1964).

c4. Studies of the Central Hydraulics Laboratory of France 1969.

c5. Law 53 of 1984 signed by President Belisario Betancur, expired without being fulfilled.

d. What needs to be done?

d1. Obtain cadastral certificates of the properties of the Canal Zone,

d2. Modify and update the Feasibility and Feasibility study,

d3. Plotting the route in 1: 10,000 scale (satellite photos),

d4. Environmental studies of the Canal Zone, including census of trees in the Zone between Coredó and Riosucio: ~ 328 feet per 492 feet on each side of the Canal line. CANATCOL undertakes the task to reforest all areas with the same number of trees cut down.

d.5 Submit the deeds to the National Planning Department, the National Infrastructure Agency (ANI), the Ministry of Transportation and Infrastructure and the National Authority of Environmental Licenses (ANLA) plans and environmental studies for approval.

d6. Obtain the necessary resources to build the work: There are several options:
a. The International Finance Corporation of the World Bank offers soft loans for regional projects if the Governors, authorized by the Assemblies of the region make the request.

b. Give in concession for a period of 30 years to a national or foreign company the redesign, financing construction, operation, maintenance of the Colombia Canal.

c. The Governor of Antioquia may request from the Antioquia Senators a new bill to replace Law 53 of 1984, signed by President Belisario Betancur by ordering the 27 Battalions of Military Engineers to do the work and the New Granada Military University do all the studies necessary to obtain the construction license.

d. Build the Colombia Interoceanic Canal.

2. Department of Chocó

The Department of Chocó is one of the 32 geopolitical divisions of Colombia, named after a tribe that inhabits the Northwest corner of Colombia, neighboring Panama. It is the only Department of Colombia with coasts in the two oceans.

Chocó has an area of 46,530 km2 and 500,000 inhabitants:
• Afro-Colombians (82.1%)
• Native Americans or Indigenous (12.7%)
• White and Mestizos (5.2%)

Chocó has 32 municipalities among which are Juradó in the Pacific, Riosucio in the Atrato river and Unguía in the Gulf of Urabá, Atlantic Ocean.

The Department of Chocó produces 47% of Colombia's gold, approximately one million Troy ounces per year. Also 100% of Platinum, the exact figure is not known since multinational mining companies export raw ore as there are no refineries in Chocó. The Department of Chocó is one of the rainiest regions in the world: Lloró receives 15,000 mm (49 feet) of rain per year. It has more than 1,000 rivers but has no pure water or electricity.

The Atrato river is the fourth largest in the world with a capacity of 176,573cubic feet/ sec. It has 466 miles in length a South-North path, drains through a delta in the Gulf of Urabá. With certain periodicity the valley of the Atrato river floods and covers with its vast waters flooding several cities. In Riosucio, the waters rise at least 10 feet high.

One of its most important tributaries is the Truandó River that is born in the Baudó Range, has an N-NE course and flows into the Atrato at the height of Riosucio. It is separated from the Pacific Ocean by the Baudó Range.

a. Resources

Presbyter Federico Cornelio Aguilar wrote a book in 1884, entitled "Colombia in the presence of the Hispano-American Republics", Imp I. Borda, (Bogotá) 1884; he quotes: "The Atrato that receives 150 tributaries and 300 navigable streams, crosses 134 leagues, of which 118 are by vapors, bathes the opulent Chocó, one of the richest countries in the world, but the most, in gold mines * and by in the middle of a short runway it communicates with the also navigable San Juan, leading east into the Pacific and that into the Atlantic."

* The geological riches of Chocó are incalculable, says M. Armando Recklus: "Australia's large alluvial deposits, which may be, in part as rich as those in Chocó, are not generally exposed to the action of rivers."

Humboldt says: "The Chocó could produce by itself more than ten thousand gold frames of laundry [sic], by populating that region, one of the most fertile in the world and the richest in gold."

M. Molein summarizes: "In the Chocó, the ground is so to speak, entirely of gold. "

The official figures are as follows, obviously they do not include illegal mining.

Platinum figures are doubtful because there is no refinery in Chocó. Chocó produces 100% of the Platinum of Colombia that vanishes like the rest of the Gold.

Gold and Platinum Production, Chocó Department
2008-2013

Total Platinum: 6,280.22 Kg, 2012,905 Troy Ounces
US $ 243,901,240

Total Gold: 126,495.29 Kg 4,066,823 Troy Ounces
US $ 5,010,325,936

Total Gold and Platinum: US $ 5,254,227,176

Based on this information, it cannot be conceived as the richest Department in Colombia that produces 47% of gold and 99.9% of platinum is in a humanitarian crisis, in the poverty of more than 67% of its inhabitants and in the extreme poverty of 9% of the population of half a million inhabitants. 60% is the unemployment figure estimated by the Catholic Bishops of the three Dioceses.

Given the riches of resources, some of the questions that we are asking include:
- What is done all the gold and platinum that vanishes and leaves nothing but scars?
- Why do children age 5 to 10 commit suicide by hunger?
- Why does it have the highest maternal and infant mortality in the Western Hemisphere?
- Why does having 1,000 rivers but not having drinking water or electricity?
- Why do the ICFES exams put schools in the last place in Chocó?

Agriculture is not possible due to the great rainfall, although a possible solution is hydroponic crops. In the areas near the coast, bananas, cassava are grown, and food used to be complemented by fishing in the rivers, however with the mining, there is a high degree of contamination with mercury and cyanide in the waters. In the town of Lloró, the Coca-Cola company is packing rainwater.

b. Communications, Infrastructure.

The transportation of the population is done mainly by canoe in the rivers. There are only two roads: one connects Quibdó with Medellín, 124 miles on which 16 hours of travel are spent. The other, Quibdó-Pereira, frequently undergoes collapses and frequently suspends circulation. The airport of Quibdó has just been remodeled.

c. Socioeconomic Indicators

In the second decade of this millennium, there is a humanitarian crisis in the Department of Chocó, which includes:
1. Maternal mortality 358: 100,000 (the highest in the Western Hemisphere). Infant mortality 110: 1000 (DANE).
2. Children from 5 to 10 years die due to hunger (RCN, 2012).
3. Malnutrition and anemia 73% (ICBF).
4. Unemployment 28.5% (DANE figure, but according to the Bishops of Chocó is 60%)
5. Minimum infrastructure.
6. Poverty rate 67% (DANE)
7. Twelve hospitals that do not have water or electricity and do not pay the personnel.
8. Education: The ICFES school exams showed that Chocó is in the last place in Colombia and Colombia is in the last place in the world.

Something needs to be done for the richest Department in Colombia, which produces more than one million ounces of gold a year, and platinum.

"Colombia is, in truth, the golden key between the Atlantic Ocean and the Pacific, key that everyone would want to hoard to open the Interoceanic Canal to which they smile and at the same time fear all the nations of the world. Colombia, that of the monster

canal, that of glorious legends, that of enormous wealth, seedbed of millions, Babylon
of commerce." (Nicolás Aristizábal Llanos, 1912).

3. Department of Antioquia: (Colombia)

Antioquia is in the northwestern part of the country. It limits to the north with the
Caribbean Sea and with the department of Córdoba; to the west with the department of
Chocó; to the east with the departments of Bolívar, Santander and Boyacá; and to the
south with the departments of Caldas and Risaralda. Its capital is the city of Medellín.

https://www.ecured.cu/Department_of_Antioquia_(Colombia)

In 2017, a population of 6,613,118 of which 79% of European origin, 16% Amerindian
and 6% African was estimated. The Afro-Colombian population living in Antioquia is
598,006 people according to the 2005 census, which represents 10.9% of the total
population.

The thesis of some students of the University of La Salle in Bogotá presented the
project for the study, construction, assembly, commissioning and control of the Atrato -
Truandó Interoceanic Canal.

In turn, the governments of Carlos Lleras Restrepo, Alfonso López Michelsen, Belisario
Betancur, Virgilio Barco and César Gaviria, in turn resumed the issue, carrying out
other studies or simply giving it new impetus. In 2010, specifically the month of
December, the Initiatives of Connection of Antioquia with the Colombian Northwest of
2010 were presented by the Government of Antioquia in agreement with the School of
Engineers of Antioquia for the BIRD Antioquia (Bank of Regional Initiatives for the
Development of Antioquia). There are the Archimedes Plan, the Mountain Highway,
hydroelectric, rail and the Interoceanic Canal.

In 2014, an investigation led by the engineer Jaime Jiménez, coordinated and led the
research group that reveals the navigability potentials of the Atrato River "We
discovered that the Atrato River is navigable throughout its route and has no
sedimentation problems." In the investigation they addressed the geological,
geomorphological, cadastral, environmental, economic, social, hydrological, hydraulic,
transport and naval components.

The most relevant results confirm the Atrato as the best river artery in terms of its flow
rate and navigable days per year without physical intervention requirements.

4.   The Colombian Interoceanic Canal Project.

Colombia has almost all the studies to build the Interoceanic Canal.

These include the following:

1. Original layout of the expedition of Engineer William Kennish in 1856.

2. Hydrometric studies carried out by commissions of the US and Colombia. The last commission directed by Belisario Ruiz Wilches, Julio Fajardo, Santiago Garavito and Leonzio González. Also, Major Añez of the Corps of Military Engineers of Colombia in 1949.

3. Prefeasibility Study of Laverde Gubert, L: Canals of Colombia 1956, (Thesis of Superior School of War, Lorenzo Codazzi Award).

4. Maps of the Atrato-Truandó Rivers on a 1: 25,000 scale by the Agustín Codazzi Geographic Institute, in 1964.

5. Study by the University of La Salle 1996.

6. Study of the School of Engineers of Antioquia 2010.

7. Atrato River Navigability Study of the Pacific Environmental Research Institute (IIAP) 2014.

The construction of the Canal requires the development of a Hydrail train parallel to the Canal, to take 60 million tons of rock from the Baudó Range to other sites.
The Colombian Canal is the only place where communication can be done at sea-level, without locks between the two oceans. 163 years ago, Kennish proposed to make two 3.0 mile-long tunnels to cross the Serranía del Baudó. The Atrato is the fourth largest river in the world with a capacity of 176,573 cubic feet / sec at the mouth, variable depth between 80 and100 feet width between 500 and 1,640 feet, speed of 2 knots per hour.

The part corresponding to the Colombian Canal measures 57 miles from Riosucio (the highest point at 137 feet above sea-level).

The 300 references on the Colombian Canal indicate that all geographic, geological, topographic, environmental, hydraulic, and sanitary studies have been done. Colombia deserves that this canal be built during our generation for the benefit of all Colombians.

What is needed for the project?

A. Trace: Trace the route of the Canal, Coredó 6.9 3333, -77.65 and. Unguia 8.25-76.98,

B. Inventory: Make the inventory of the trees of said path. It is estimated that they are worth US $ 3.5 billion. (Sanin, 2003)

C. Strategies:

1. To grant the highest priority, authorize the Executive to order the National Financial Corporation to give the State guarantee to the National and International Credit.

2. Authorize the issuance of bonds and shares for the construction and operation of the Canal.

3. It is essential to use the great height of the Pacific tides that rise 13 feet high to generate electricity for the entire Department of Chocó.

4. Order 27 Battalions of Military Engineers to do the work.

5. All dredges and heavy equipment seized by the Police from illegal miners must be handed over to the armed forces and used by the military engineers to continuously dredge the rivers and maintain the depth of the Colombian Canal. The extracted sand can be used to raise the level of the new ports above 20 feet high, and thus prevent damage caused by flooding.

6. It is urgent to ban the export of platinum ore, which is carried by airplanes to foreign refineries. Condoto must have its own refinery and employ the people of Chocó who live in misery amid this mineral wealth that only leaves 17.5% of taxes.

7. The Colombia Canal Zone, should have a cooperative like Migros from Switzerland, to take advantage of all-natural resources, promote crops and market them.

D. Specifications

A two-way canal is needed for Ultra Large Container ships (ULCS) which will be 85% of the Merchant Fleet in 2030. The Colombian Canal has a total of 107 miles distributed as follows: 16 miles from Coredó to the Serranía del Baudó; 33.5 miles to Riosucio; 57 miles from Riosucio to Unguía. The deep-water port in the Pacific Ocean will be in Curiché, Municipality of Juradó at 7 ° North Latitude.

There is a need to make an open pit cut in the Serranía del Baudó of 15,748 feet long, 492 feet wide at the base and 92 feet deep. This region constitutes 85% of the Canal construction work, it must be attacked on two fronts.

The current of the canal is 2 miles per hour. The Atlantic tide rises 3.2 feet in the Atrato. The Pacific tide rises 13 feet and can reach the Atrato lakes. The hydraulic studies were done by the EU-Colombia Joint Commission in 1949. Subsequently by the Hydraulic Central Laboratory of France in 1969. The report by Engineer Jean Bottagisio, Director of the study stated that there was no problem.
The description of the route is found in the Kennish book of 1855, and there are two laws, Law 53 of 1964 and Law 53 of 1984 to make the canal.

E. Design of the canal.

The ideal design of the Canal will be a design with radius curves of more than 33,000 feet (10,000 meters):

The Canal will begin in Coredó (6.9 3333, -77.65) in the Pacific. The open cut will be made at the intermediate point between the Curiché lagoon of the Curiché river and the north of the source of the Coredó river. It is directed towards the NE.

The Baudo range will be reached (3 miles from the beach). It will cross through an open cut of 15,748 feet through the basalt mountain. The line will cross the Serranía de Baudo and continue directly to a site 6.8 miles (11 km) north of Riosucio to enter the Atrato River east of the Peyé River and the Cienagas de Tumaradó, of the Katíos National Park and end at the Tarena pipe, Municipality of Unguía.

The option of following the course of the Truandó and Atrato Rivers proposed in the nineteenth and twentieth centuries is not valid now when the ships are gigantic, difficult to maneuver and make curves, it is better a route with few and very wide curves.

It is necessary to draw the Canal line to demarcate a 950 feet (300 m) wide corridor along the line, to make the forest inventory, price it and submit it for auction.

Both Kennish (1855) and Michler (1861) proposed to excavate a tunnel 3 miles (4.8 km) long to cross the Baudo Range. Nowadays an open cut is needed in the Baudo range. The slopes must be calculated. The prism must have a base 492 feet (150 m) wide. The cut is like the Corinth Canal that was made in the 19th century when Nobel had not invented dynamite.

As mentioned earlier, there are jumbo machines with pneumatic hammers or the laser to make the perforations and fill them with Expansive Cements that fracture the rock without explosions.

To flatten the bed of the canal a basalt slicer manufactured by Vermeer model T1655 Commander 3 is used. Another possibility in drilling with Electric Pulses (info @ terracoh- age.com.com,j.griffin@terracoh-age.com, John Griffin TerraCOH, Inc. Tel 612-201-6896)

The design of the six camps was pointed out by Kennish in 1855. East and West of the Baudo range to cut the mountain from two fronts. Electric generators will be necessary to allow 24-hour construction in three 8-hour shifts, six days a week.
To move 100 million tons of basaltic rock, you need a 15.5 mile (25 km) railway that runs from Coredó in the NE direction to the end of the mainland of the Serranía's extension.
There you must transfer the slabs to the banks of the canal. The ideal if it were electric or with hydrogen cell engines, side dump wagons to move the Baudo basaltic rocks

and transport them to the banks of the Canal to protect them. At the end of the construction of the Canal, the line could be extended to Antioquia, Risaralda and Quindío and in a second stage to Guayaquil and Maracaibo.

The design will include the following:
1. Two deep water ports in Unguía and Coredó with all facilities.
2. International airport in Cabo Marzo.
3. Master plan for the development of an intelligent city for 100,000 inhabitants with an industrial zone, railway center, heavy machinery factories, shipyard, etc.
4. Design of the 250 MW tidal energy plant in Juradó with 13 feet (4.2 m) high tides.
5. Design of the 150 KW geothermal power plant at the Juradó, Nuquí and Unguía hot springs must do to generate electricity for Chocó, the Canal, the railroad and the new industries.
6. Two cement plants in Cabo Tiburon and Napipi.

Corinth Canal, Greece

High energy laser greater than one megawatt on AVA-7A1 vehicles, to cut 33 feet (10 m) of basalt per hour.

There is a US patent from Mr. Martin A. Stuart # 8220965 of July 2012 for a High Energy Laser:

Laser energy source device and method

Martin A. Stuart

<table>
<tr><td>Abstract

      🖼

</td><td>Overview
› Abstract
Drawings
Description
Claims</td></tr>
</table>

Go

Patent number: 8220965
Filing date: Apr 20, 2010
Issue date: Jul 17, 2012
Application number: 12/763,437

"Systems with 1,000 KW (1 MW) rays have the ability to vaporize 1 inch (2.5 cm) in diameter through 9.8 feet (3 meters) of rock per second. This would allow the cutting of 52 feet (16 m) through 328 feet (100 m) of rock in a span of five hours. (Speed levels will be increased in direct proportion with each corresponding megawatt increase). "
Stuart, Martin A. (Burbank, CA, USA)
Currently the most powerful Laser is from the US Air Force with 150 KW.

Fig. 1. Russian Beriev A-60 (modified IL-76MD) with **HEL** turret and nose mounted radar. 1.1-MW HEL turret, 2 — radar for detecting aerial targets, 3 — compartment for 2.1 MW turboalternator. Photograph taken at Taganrog Yuznyi Airport in May 2011 by O. Ziminov, RovSpotters Team.

The United States Navy has a 100 KW Laser that it has just used to destroy cannon or mortar bullets, pilotless planes, missiles and small ships.
The Russian Air Force has a 1.1 MW Laser installed in an airplane.

Russian Air Laser

Israel uses a 700 KW Laser to shoot down enemy rockets.

F. Budget

Assuming a cost of US $ 100 million per km (0.6 mile), 172 km (107 miles) of the Colombia Canal would cost USD $ 17,200 million. The work can be done on six fronts in a period of 24 to 48 months.

Financing

CANATCOL, AP requires the highest priority and the guarantee of THE NATIONAL FINANCIAL CORPORATION, for the issuance of bonds, stocks and international loans.
The sale of timber from the canal area is estimated to provide USD $ 3.5 billion.

What we have?

- The most valuable corner of America.
- The only site in the hemisphere where an Interoceanic Canal can be made at sea level for Ultra Large Container Ships.
- A private Association of the owners of the Canal Zone, CANATCOL, AP that wishes to open the Interoceanic Canal.
- 1855 Description of the W. Kennish, F. Kelley route (New York).
- 1861 Report of the Mission of Lieutenant N. Michler (Washington, DC).
- 1949 Study of the Atrato-Truandó Canal of the Governor Canal Panama (Law 280/1949 USA).
- 1970 US Government Commission Interoceanic Canal.
- 1964 Engineering, geology, and soil studies.
- 1969 Central Hydraulics Laboratory of France.
- 2014 Navigability Atrato River Studies.

What has been done?

- LAW # 53 of 1964 whereby plans and economic studies were contracted with two New York companies Tippetts- Abbett-McCarthy-Stratton and R. Nathan.
- Law # 53 of 1984 Ordered the construction of the Canal.
- Decree 0926 of 1996 contract with Nathan of New York feasibility studies. They concluded that they should wait to finish the expansion of the Panama Canal.

What needs to be done?

A partner or partners to form a Consortium that:
- Redesign the plans.
- Complete the environmental studies.
- Form a Limited Liability Corporation (LLC) with CANATCOL as a Majority partner.

- Take inventory of trees.
- Trace the route of the Canal,
- Finance the investment with bond issuance.
- Build and operate the Canal for 30 years.

What could be done?

Option 1.
- Proclaim a new law that orders the Military Engineers to build the Canal.
- Finance the open cut of the Baudo range with the sale of trees.
- Finance the rest with bond issuance.

Option 2.
Santiago Pérez Triana proposed in 1915 in London to grant a Multinational Engineering Company in concession to do the work, finance and operate the Canal for a defined number of years.

The issuance of bonds may be a convenient option to meet the requirements. Foreign financing and international support could be explored with the following countries and organizations: Spain, Switzerland, China, France, Japan, Holland, South Korea, Qatar, Singapore, United Kingdom, USA, European Union.

The Minister of Foreign Affairs of Japan Fumio Kishida considered that the width of the Panama Canal is insufficient for its vessels. (Wall Street Journal, 2014). Japan is in an energy crisis due to the destruction of the Fukushima reactors by the Tsunami. Japan imports 98% of oil, and 90% of Coal. Japan through its organizations JICA (Bilateral Cooperation Agency) and the execution of Japan's ODA (Official Development Assistance) can develop negotiations. It must also be included in the FTA (Free Trade Agreement) that is currently being carried out with Japan.

Holland could also do the feasibility study with the Dutch companies Royal Haskoning-DHV and Ecorys as done with Nicaragua, due to their experience and knowledge in maritime transport and the manufacture of cranes for large ports.

The European Union has programs and economic resources for humanitarian crisis problems, which is the reality today in Chocó.

Reasons to make the Colombia Interoceanic Canal

1. The Ultra Large Container Ships (ULCS) of 18,000 TEU's will be 85% of the Merchant Fleet in 2030.
2. The route of the Interoceanic Canal of Colombia is the only region in America where a Canal can be made at sea-level. (US Interoceanic Canal Commission, 1970).
3. The Bay of Humboldt and the Gulf of Urabá are protected areas against Hurricanes.
4. The distance between the two Oceans is only 172 kilometers (107 miles).

5. It is the most profitable business that can be done: Investment $ 17 billion. It produces $ 6 billion a year.
6. The Colombia Interoceanic Canal will create a development pole of the greatest importance for Colombia and the region.
7. After finishing it, there are several projects that will be possible with the income flow of the Colombia Interoceanic Canal: Deep water ports, coastal railroad, heavy industry factories, shipyards.
8. National will, political support and the desire to contribute to Pacific Development are needed.

The world merchant fleet is growing. The shipping company Maersk, one of the largest in the world announced that it has to increase the distance by 2000 kilometers and use the Suez Canal. This Canal has just built the second route to increase traffic from 45 to 96 ships per day and increasing revenue for Egypt from $ 5.5 billion to $ 9.5 billion a year.

According to Professor Jean-Paul Rodrigue "Bottlenecks of global maritime shipping have been, for decades, the object of geostrategic considerations as obligatory points of passage. The connectivity they provide is related to the reduction of maritime shipping distances for international trade and the convergence of shipping services. The setting of transshipment hubs, which support and expand the connectivity of maritime shipping, has been particularly active around major maritime bottlenecks since they are natural points of convergence. This usually involves feeder services towards smaller ports, relays connecting deep-sea services towards different maritime ranges or interlining, supporting different port of call configurations along a similar maritime range". (Rodrigue, 2019).

Assumptions for Feasibility Study Colombia Interoceanic Canal

A. Pass a vessel of> 14,000 TEU every hour = 24 a day to $ US 300,000 $ 100,000 = $ 2,400,000 x 365 = $ 876,000,000

B. Two ships pass every hour (48 per year) = $ 1,752,000,000 per year.

C. 4 ships pass every hour (96 per year) = $ 3,504,000,000

Cost of operations $ 2 million per year. Investment US $ 13,450,150,000 plus interest 4% $ 140,160,000 = $ 13,590,310, can be paid in 10 years.

Feasibility Study to include:

1. This infrastructure investment will create a continuous flow of dollars. 40% will be dedicated to pay the debt, the rest for development of infrastructure of the Canal in order to improve their operational conditions, (pure water, septic tanks, industrial

development: metalworking factory of heavy industry, dredgers, cranes; shipyard construction of tugs and barges, and port infrastructure among other developments).

2. Plans: Update the plans and economic studies of the Colombia Interoceanic Canal, on Route 25A, made in New York in 1964.

3. Soil Studies: Complete the soil studies of the Serranía del Baudó that have not been done.

4. Ecological Research: Do the ecological research necessary to obtain the environmental license.

5. Deeds and Plans: Submit the deeds and plans and a 3D video of the model to the National Planning Department for approval.

6. Construction: Build the Colombian Canal, manage and operate.

7. Road Infrastructure: Finish the Pan-American Highway, South route: Animas – Nuqui- Bahia Solano- Jurado- Palos de Letra- Panama.

8. Power Plant: Build the 200 MW tidal power plant in Juradó, Chocó.

9. Cement Factories: Build two cement factories in Cabo Tiburon and Napipí.

10. Heavy Equipment Factories: Build a heavy equipment factory, railway equipment and a shipyard in the Pacific.

11. Refineries: Build and put into operation under the control of the Banco de la República a Gold and Platinum refinery.

12. Engine Factories: Build an engine factory operated by hydrogen cells with Platinum membranes.

13. Wood Factories: Build a company to process wood owned by CANATCOL, AP.

14. Staple Food Factory: Build a fishing company with fishing vessels in the Pacific and the Atlantic, owned by CANATCOL, AP. Seafood baler.

15. Education: Canal University to educate the workers of the canal and their families, to include faculties of:
- Engineering sciences: civil engineering, hydraulics, systems, mechanics, naval, administration, technical school of pilots, canal operators, dredgers.
- Medical sciences: medicine, nursing, school for midwives, nutrition, pharmacy.

16. Health: three III level hospital connected to health posts in 27 municipalities by Telemedicine, and a Tropical Research Institute to take care of the workers of the canal.

CANATCOL, AP organized a forum that was held in Quibdó, Chocó from January 18 to 20, 2018 at the Auditorium of the Technological University of Chocó. A partner is being sought to redesign, finance, build and operate the Interoceanic Canal for several years. Engineering companies from all over the world were invited to participate in the workshop. Advisors from the University of Liege, Belgium consider it a great opportunity for investment and development of the Pacific Coast of Colombia.

Income

According to Reuters, the Suez Canal produced $ 853.7 million between March and April 2017. The Panama Canal produced $ 1119.5 million from January to June 2017. The toll of the Panama Canal produced gains of 19.7% in the first half of 2017 (https: // ph.invertalia.net/.../panama-canal)

Financing

The Interoceanic Canal could be financed through the following ideas:
1. Sale in international auction of fine wood of the Canal Zone.
2. National, International Bank Loans (National Financial Corporation Guarantees, Bogotá).
3. Colombian Association of Private Equity Funds.
4. Issuance of bearer Bonds (those issued by Egypt to expand Suez Canal were sold in 6 hours).
5. International Finance Corporation (IFC of the World Bank) Y. Quiroz Tel (571) 319-2330. Loans for regional projects must be requested by Governors).

Colombia Interoceanic Canal Costs

1. Chocó Canal Zone
172,000 km x 300 m = 51,600,000 m2 has a value USD $ 1,000,000 / m2 =
USD $ 51,600,000,000,000

2. Canal zone trees $ 3.5 billion dollars

3. Wood from the rivers Truandó and Salaquí $ 7 million.

4. Construction of the Interoceanic Canal of Chocó
172 Km to $ 100 million per Kilometer =
USD $ 17.2 billion.

5. Projection of income with an average of $ 300,000 per toll 48 daily crossings

x 1-day USD $ 14,000,000
x 30 days USD $ 432,000,000
365 days USD $ 5,256,000,000

7. Operation and maintenance expenses 5%
1-day USD $ 700,000
30 days USD $ 2,100,000
365 days USD $ 255,500,000

8. Daily net USD $ 13,300,000
Net x 30 days USD $ 411,000,000
Net 365 days UD $ 5,006,000

The Concessionaires will receive 25% of the income and CANATCOL must receive 75% of the income for payment of the debt and for infrastructure costs. With the income from tolls, the debt can be paid in 30 years.

12. CONCLUSIONS

A new Interoceanic Canal is needed in the Americas to plan for the near future given the projections for 2030 that 85% of the World Merchant Fleet will include Ultra Large Container Ships of 400 meters in length and 18,000 TEU.

1.The Private Association CANATCOL, AP (Law 1508/2012) was constituted by the owners of the Canal Zone (Law 70.1993). CANATCOL represents the communities that own the Canal area in the Municipalities of Juradó, Riosucio, Unguía and Turbo. The extension between the two oceans is 107 miles (172 km).

Most of the land is alluvial, easy to dig. The most challenging section is to cross the lower area of the Baudó range of 951 feet (290 m) above sea-level, with an open-cut cut of 15,748 feet (4,800 m) long, 492 feet (150 m) wide at the base and 92 feet (28 m) deep to allow Ultra Large Ship Pass (ULCS), of more than 18,000 TEU.

2. Market:
There is enough demand for the merchant marine with an increasing size of ships. The Foreign Minister of Japan, Mr. Fumio Kishida, wrote to the President of Panama complaining that "the new locks are not wide enough for the passage of 600,000 Ton ships."

3. Competition:
The Colombian Canal will be a complement to the Panama Canal, to avoid the bottleneck of ships travelling from the East to the West and vice versa.

4. Team:
The Board of Directors of CANATCOL, AP is made up of representatives of the ethnic communities. The Government of Colombia requires a law to exempt the construction of the canal from all taxes and for a period of 10 years for new companies that are installed in the Department of Chocó. The Government of Colombia is also being requested to replace Law 53 of 1984 and order the 27 Battalions of Military Engineers to build the Interoceanic Canal with advice from the Water Center of UNESCO-Latin America, or with a School of Roads, Channels and Ports (Law 24 of 1959).

5. Funds:
It is estimated that the construction of the Canal will cost US $ 17,200,000,000 and that it can take between three to five years doing the work from six work fronts, with three eight-hour shifts. Considering that the income of the Suez Canal with the expansion built by the military engineers of Egypt in one year, revenues increased from $ 5.5 to $ 9.5 billion a year. The Panama Canal in the first 6 months of 2017 had an income exceeding one billion dollars. It is projected that the revenues of the Interoceanic Channel of Colombia will pay the debt in a short term.

6. Mission:
CANATCOL, AP seeks to end the humanitarian crisis denounced by the Catholic Bishops and confirmed by the Office of the Ombudsman and the United Nations. CANATCOL, AP respects the customs and traditions of the owners, seeks to improve health, nutrition, education, and housing conditions. Provide the Department of Chocó with the infrastructure and electric power necessary for the development of industries, to provide pure water to all inhabitants, to build wastewater treatment plants to prevent damage to nature.

7. Legal structure:
The Legal Structure of the Private Association is based on the law of the Republic of Colombia # 1508/2012, which allows the creation of such companies for infrastructure.

8. Headquarters:
The headquarters of CANATCOL is in Quibdó, Department of Chocó, Colombia, although it is expected that in the future other branches may be opened in Colombia and abroad.

**THE UNKNOWN TREASURE
FOR THIS GENERATION OF COLOMBIAN.**

The new generations of Colombians do not remember the history of the Interoceanic Canal. There is enough information for the Government of Colombia, and the Executive and Legislative powers to think about the urgency of building the Colombian Canal at sea-level. In addition to providing a great service to world trade, Colombia will receive immense income that will raise GDP to 11% annually.

The pacification of Western Colombia requires the militarization of criminal redoubts and the development of unmet needs of the population related mainly in the sectors creating sources of jobs to end 60% unemployment reported by the Bishops of Chocó in 2015.

To begin, the Afro-Colombian bank must file the bill to replace Law 53 of 1984 that expired without being fulfilled. The Afro Descendants Bank has a debt of honor with their fellow citizens to celebrate the Colombian Bicentennial of Independence, filing the bill on July 20, 2019.

The President and Vice President of Colombia in charge of Infrastructure, should give top priority to the megaproject that will put the name of Colombia in the geography and history of the World, as the largest contribution of the present administration.

On September 25, 2013, celebrated 500 years of the discovery of the South Sea (Pacific Ocean) by Vasco Núñez de Balboa guided by the son of Chief Panquiaco. The expedition departed from Santa María la Antigua del Darién (the first city established in

Colombia on the banks of the Tarena pipe, where Núñez de Balboa became interim governor), Municipality of Unguía (Chocó) one of the mouths of the delta of the fourth largest river in the world, the Atrato River. His expedition crossed the shortest area of the isthmus of Panama and arrived to the South Sea, named Pacific Ocean in 1520.

New generations of Colombians are unaware of the hidden treasure that lies abandoned and forgotten by everyone, including the country's leaders. The remote Chocó, which has no pure water despite the fact that it rains 12.5 meters (41 feet) a year, has no electricity despite having 1,000 rivers, has no infrastructure despite having rich gold and platinum mines, is starving to death amidst incredible amounts of wealth, due to the lack of vision of Colombian leaders.

160 years ago, a New York millionaire Frederick M. Kelley sent seven expeditions to seek interoceanic communication in New Granada (now Colombia). On the fifth expedition in 1854 the Civil Engineer Captain William Kennish found the Atrato-Truandó route, beginning at 7 ° North Latitude in the Coriché Estuary in the Pacific Ocean and ending in the Gulf of Urabá in the Caribbean Sea.

There are 172 kilometers (107 miles) between the two oceans: 26 km (16 miles) are from the Serranía del Baudó, where the lowest pass is 280 meters (918 feet) above sea-level. Kennish proposed to make two 4.8 km (3 mile) tunnels to pass the ships of that time. Crossing the basalt barrier of the Baudó range, you reach the valley of the Nerqua river that flows into the Truandó. Captain Kennish and his expedition were overwhelmed with the fertility of these two valleys that could feed a million workers that may be needed to make the Canal.

The 54 km (33.5 miles) Truandó River current that flows into the Atrato, in Riosucio the highest part of the Canal at 47 meters (154 feet) from sea-level. The journey in the majestic Atrato has 92 km (57 miles) whose undulations must be rectified to reach the Gulf of Urabá. 28 meters (92 feet) deep are required to allow the passage of modern Ultra Large Container Ships (ULCS) of more than 400 m. of length.

That is the treasure of Colombia: an interoceanic route at sea-level, without locks for new sea giants that carry containers from one ocean to another.
The toll revenue of the future Canal will be of the order of US $ 6,000 million a year that will be devoted to health, education and infrastructure of the region.

From Riosucio, the port can be communicated with the rest of the country, the railway and the Pan-American Highway can pass under the waters as in New York and other parts of the world.

In 1964, the Minister of Works Tomás Castrillón Muñoz submitted the bill to build the Canal. The law was passed. The Agustín Codazzi Geographic Institute (IGAC) lifted the Atrato-Truandó Topographic map at a scale of 1: 25,000. The plans were contracted with the Tippetts-Abbett-McCarthy-Stratton Engineers Company. They recommended nuclear explosions that were obviously not accepted. Economic studies were done by Robert R. Nathan and associates of New York.

In 1970 the Commission of the United States for the Interoceanic Canal, studied thirty possible sites to join the two oceans and concluded that the only one where an interoceanic route can be made at sea-level, without locks, is in Colombia. This route # 25 was studied intensively.

In 1984, 35 years ago, Senator Daniel Palacios Martínez introduced Bill # 53 to build the Canal, which was approved. The Geographical Society of Colombia in 1985 with the coordination of Colonel (R) Civil Engineer Rafael Convers Pinzón conducted the I Forum on the Atrato-Truandó Canal. The conclusions were positive; however, nothing was done, except the publication of the Book by Alberto Mendoza Morales, et. all (1996) on the Atrato-Truandó Canal.

Summarizing, a national purpose is needed: it is essential to make a new law that includes the Canal Zone. The following steps should be followed:

1. The Agustín Codazzi Geographic and Cadastral Institute must deliver the cadastral records of the owners of the Canal Zone with deeds until June 30, 2019.

2. The ICA must inventory the natural resources that will be sold to the highest bidder.

3. A law is required to declare a duty-free Zone to the Canal Zone and to the companies that settle in it for a period of 10 years. The Ministry of Transportation must make the regulatory decree of the law.

4. In November 2015, the Colombian Private Channel Association, CANATCOL, AP was established.

5. Manage loans with national and international credit institutions.

6. Give the guarantees of the State.

7. Open the international competition to concession for 30 years the construction, operation and maintenance of the Colombian Canal at sea-level.

8. Prepare a new generation of Colombian Engineers for Hydraulic, Environmental, Sanitary, Electrical, Geomancy, Business Administration, Railway Engineering studies. Experts are needed in the construction of roads, canals and ports, in the handling of heavy equipment, in the cyber control of the canal, etc.

Colombia urgently requires this megaproject to end poverty and join the first world countries. The Colombian Canal will create a development pole for the mechanical metal industry, shipyards, repair and construction workshops for railway equipment, cement factories, free zone, tax incentives for new industries that are built in the Canal Zone.

The construction of two seaports in Coredó (Chocó) in the Pacific and a deep-water port in Unguía will facilitate the development of infrastructure providing pure water, electricity, housing, hospitals, schools, markets, warehouses, workshops, warehouses and airports.

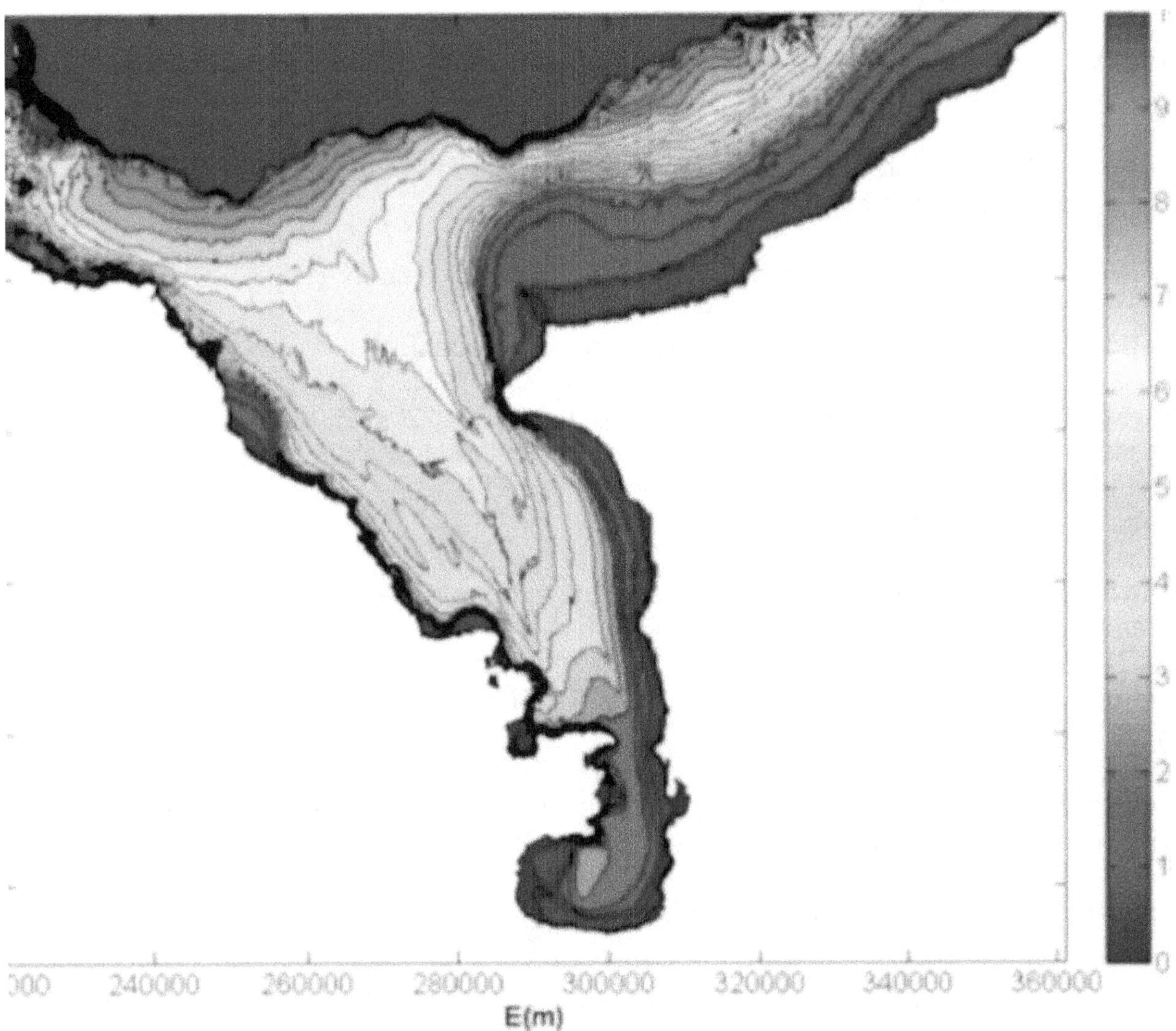

Blanco Libreros JF, Londoño Mesa MH: "South Caribbean Expedition: Antioquia and Chocó coastal" -tesis.udea.edu.co, Medellín. Colombia 2016

13. BIBLIOGRAPHY

CANAL ATRATO PRIVATE ASSOCIATION, COLOMBIA (CANATCOL, AP)
A "NASA Project" for Colombia: Build the Atrato-Truandó Canal!
EIR 1985; 12 (34): 20-29

Acevedo de la Torre E: Atrato-Truandó Nature and Tec Interoceanic Canal, Bogotá 1950

Aguilar FC: "Colombia in the presence of the Hispanic-American Republics", Imp I. Borda, (Bogotá) 1884.

Airiau A: Canal Interocéaniques par l'Isthme de Darien, Nouvelle Granada (Amérique du Sud) Colonization, Paris 1860.

Alfredo, T. Brother. Interoceanic Channel is prospected at the level of the Atrato Canal-Truandó between the projects / 1968.

Alfredo, T. Brother. Canal Atrato-San Juan o Canal del Chocó / 1968.

Alfredo, T. Brother. Canal del Atrato- Truandó Bol Sogecol 1967, 25 (93-94).

Alvarez Lleras, J. The Atrato Canal, Bol Sogecol 1966; 128-129 (2)
American interoceanic canals; a list of references in the New York Public Library
https://archive.org/stream/ americaninteroce00newy /
americaninteroce00newy_djvu.txt

Arango Lopez, M.O. et al: Shocked perspectives for its development, Thesis University of Engineering, Antioquia, 1986.

Armenta, A.L. The Interoceanic Canal Atrato-Truandó is an urgent need. Sogecol bowl 1939; 6 (2,3).

Armenta, A.L: The Atrato-Truandó Interoceanic Canal is an unplayable need Memorial of the General Staff, Num. 3, 1940.

Armenta, A.L. The Colombian Interoceanic Canal / 1948.

Aguirre Serrano J.G. About a new Interoceanic Canal. Magazine
Armed Forces, Vol. 20 No. 59 Jan.- Mar. (1970).

Agudelo G.M. The Caribbean area and the Atrato-Truandó Canal. Armed Forces Magazine, Vol. 42 No. 122 Jan.-Mar. (1987).

Angel Sanin G.A. The geopolitical and strategic importance of the Atrato-Truandó / School Interoceanic Channel Superior of War Thesis.

Arango Lopez Martha Olga: Shocked perspectives for its development Thesis Engineering School of Antioquia, Faculty of Civil Engineering Envigado 1986.

Armenta, Antonio Luis "The Atrato-Truandó Interoceanic Canal is an unplayable need, Memorial of the General Staff, No. 3 (Mar. 1940).

Asher K: Black and Green: Afro- Colombians, Development, and Nature in the Pacific Lowlands Duke University Press, 2009.

Atlantic-Pacific Interoceanic Canal Study Commission
Author: United States. Atlantic-Pacific Interoceanic Canal Study Commission. Seven volumes, Washington, DC 1970.

Bahamón Dussán, A. The geopolitics of the Atrato-Truandó channel. Sogecol Bowl 1997, 41 (125).

Bateman, A. The Atrato Canal. Publications Group of the Ministry of Public Works, 1985.

Bateman Durán, Jaime D: Comparison of Atrato-San Miguel and Atrato-Truandó projects Annals of Engineering Bogotá vol. 92, no. 824 (Oct.-Dec.,1984).

Blanco Libreros, JF; Londoño Mesa, MH: "South Caribbean Expedition: Antioquia and Chocó coastal "-tesis.udea.edu.co, Medellín. Colombia 2016.

Brissón J, Francisco Javier Vergara and Velasco (Tr) Reconnaissance of Atrato-Truandó Sea-Level Canal Route. Exploration in El Alto Chocó, Bogotá 1905 2nd ed. BiblioLife, 2010.

Burdiol, M: Civil Engineer: Exploration dans l'Isthme de Darién Canalization par **Cullen E** Isthmus of Darien ship channel, with history of the Scotch Colony of Darien, London 1853.

Zone Channel Governor (1944-1948: Mehaffey) Special Report of the Governor of the Panama Canal on the Atrato-Truandó Canal Route: Under Public Law 280, 79th Congress, 1st Session. The Governor, 1949.

Zone Channel Dept. of Operation and Maintenance. Special Engineering Division Publisher. Department of Operations and Maintenance, Special Engineering Division, 1948.

Zone Channel Dept. of Operation and Maintenance. Special Engineering Division Modified Plan, Reconnaissance of Atrato-Truandó Sea-Level Canal Route Contributor. Publisher Department of Operations and Maintenance, Special Engineering Division, 1948.

Zone Channel Dept. of Operation and Maintenance. Special Engineering Division **Atrato-Truandó Route: Hydrography of the Lower Atrato River** (Special Canal Study - 1949). Department of Operations and Maintenance, Special Engineering Division, 1948.

Cárdenas Jaramillo, V. Bill on the Atrato-Truandó channel. Bol Sogecol 1983, 36 (118).

Cárdenas, Jaramillo, V. Bill on the Atrato-Truandó canal, Bol Sogecol 1983; 36 (118).

Carlos V, Royal Cedula giving power, instruction, ordinances to Pedrarias Dávila PARES, Archivo de Indias PATRONATO, 26, R.5 1513.
Carvajal, G. Interoceanic canalization by Chocó, 1914.

Castañeda Acevedo, P R: National strategy to develop the Colombian river environment based on future river interconnection channels generated by the Atrato, Putumayo and Magdalena rivers, Bogotá: Esdegue 2009.

Castrillón Dussan, R; **Escobar Olaya, GA**: National Navy ship services on the Atrato and Meta rivers, Bogotá: Superior War School, ESG Thesis 2013.

Castrillón Muñoz, T: Canal del Atrato exhibition of reasons for Project of the Ministry of Public Works, Bogotá, 1964.

Castrillón Muñoz, T: The Atrato Canal, Rev Javeriana 1964, 61: 305.

Castrillón Muñoz, T: A work to benefit a great emporium of wealth: the Atrato Canal, 1967.

Castro AD: The Portuguese in Hawaii Faces and Masks - Issues 378-391 - Google Books Resulthttps: //books.google.com.co/books? Id ... – 1906.

Cifuentes Ramírez, Laurentino (TN): The Atrato Canal, Armed Forces Magazine, 1970; 20 (60): 477-494.

Convers Pinzón, R: Possible financing of the Atrato-Truandó channel for its construction in ten years. Bol Sogecol 1979; 34 (114).

Convers Pinzón, R: Something else about the Atrato-Truandó Colombia Channel, follows the ostrich policy. Bol Sogeocol 1982; 36 (117).

Convers Pinzón, R: The Atrato-Truandó Interoceanic Canal and the Atrato Hydroelectric can change the fate of the country. Sogeocol 1984-1985; 37 (119-120).

Convers, Finch R: Atrato-Truandó Channel. El Dorado of the year 2000. Bol Sogeocol 1986; 38 (121).

Convers, Pinzón R: Good news about the Atrato Canal "Canal Atrato-Truandó" Bol Sogeocol 1988-1989; 39 (122).

Convers Pinzón, R: What about the Panama Canal and the Chocó Canal. Armed Forces Magazine, Vol. 42 No. 122 Jan.-Mar. (1987).

Convers Pinzón, R: The Canal of Colombia and that of Panama. Sogecol Bowl 1975, 29 (107).

Convers Pinzón, R. The Colombian Channel and the Panama Canal, 1975.
Convers Pinzón, R. Tunnel project to cross the Serranía de Baudo between the Pacific Ocean and the Atrato River, ACORE Magazine 1986; 52.

Serrano Corredor, A. Mare Nostrum / 1999.

Serrano Corredor, Alfonso. "Atrato-Truandó Interoceanic Canal." Magazine "Armada 1988; 50.

Corredor Muñoz, E: Geopolitical Vision of an Interoceanic Canal. 60 Apr-Jun (1970).

Costales Samaniego A, Webster McBride F, Peñ herrera de Costales P: Human ecology of route 25 (Atrato-Truandó) region, Chocó, Colombia Battelle Memorial Institute, Columbus Laboratories, 1970 – Colombia.

Darien Papers: A selection of original letters and Official Documents relating to the establishment of a colony at Darien by the company of Scotland Trading to Africa and the Indies Edinburgh 1849.

Davis, CH: Report of the Interoceanic canals and railroads between the Atlantic and Pacific Oceans. Washington Gov Print Off 1867 https://babel.hathitrust.org/cgi/ pt? Id = hvd.32044086969516; view = 1up; se

Duque Escobar, G. Colombia looks at the Pacific Basin. (2011), at: http: //www.bdigital.unal.edu.co/4102/1/ gonzaloduqueescobar.201151.pdf

Duque Escobar, G. A "green railroad" to articulate the seas of Colombia, at: http: //www.bdigital.unal.edu.co/8429/1/ gonzaloduqueescobar.201243.pdf

Duque Escobar, G. The Coffee Railroad by the North of Tolima for the Intermodality of Colombia.https: // scholar.google.com/scholar? as_ylo = 2016 & q = channel + atrato & hl = en & as_sd t = 0.10

Joint Session of Assemblies of Caldas and Tolima, Friday, April 29, 2016, Fresno, Tolima - http: // www.bdigital.unal.edu.co/51663/#sthash. 59Fda6ZU.dpuf

Escobar, F. The Atrato Canal. Bowl Sogecol 1936, 3 (2).

Flachat J: Notes sur I flew from Darien et sur the configuration of the Sun au point that I an interocéanique channel between the Rio Grande de Darien et l'Atrato, Paris 1866.

FOREIGN RELATIONS OF THE UNITED STATES, 1948, THE WESTERN HEMISPHERE, VOLUME IX
Agreement by the Colombian Government to preliminary reconnaissance of the Atrato–Truandó: interoceanic canal route, The Secretary of the Army (Royall) to the Secretary of State, Washington, March 3, 1948.
Friede, J. El Atrato as an access road to the Pacific. Armed Forces Magazine, Vol. 9 No. 27 Jul.-Aug. (1964).

Gomez, G.M. Social Studies Magazine-Magazine No. 03 | Elements de ... res.uniandes.edu.co ›Magazine No. 03.

Gómez, J: Sea-level Canal of Chocó, Colombia. In 1970 after studying 30 possible sites for an interoceanic sea-level canal for 250,000 tons ship canal, the USA Commission
issuu.com/...z/docs/ canal_of_colombia__8b09e191d22020

Gómez, JG., Baldwin, CG:
Interoceanic Channel AT LEVEL OF THE SEA ATRATO-TRUANDÓ, COLOMBIA
http://issuu.com/jimgomez/docs/ CANATCOL_presenta / 1

Gómez, JG: Canal de Colombia por Jim Gómez - issuuhttps: //issuu.com/jimgomez/docs/ canal_de_colombia_andm

González Escobar, L.F. He collided in the historical cartography: from uncertain territory to the Department of a country called Colombia, Bol. Cult Bibliog (BLAA), Bogotá, 1996; 43.

Governor of the Panama Canal, Special canal study - 1949, Atrato-Truandó route. "This special report supersedes all references to the Atrato-Truandó? Canal route contained in Report of the Governor of the Panama Canal, dated November 21, 1947, under Public Law 280, 79th Congress, 1st session."

Greiff Moreno, C. of. The dry Canal: passage from sea to sea, a viable solution with a national benefit / 1987.

Gutiérrez Navarro, C. The channel of America: Panama in the conquest, the colony, the independence and the secession, Atrato-Truandó Thesis Bogota 1951.

Holguín Pardo, L. Conceptual design of the Atrato-Truandó / 1996 interoceanic river bridge.

Humboldt A Von: Political Essay on the Kingdom of New Spain, translated from French by John Black, London 1811, book 1 Cap II: 30-31.

Humboldt, Friedrich Heinrich Alexander, Freiherr Von. General considerations of the possibility of joindre la mer du Sud à L'océan Atlantique. (In his: Essai politique sur le royaume de la Nouvelle-Espagne.
Paris, 1811. 8th. v. 1, ch. 2.) HTY.

Humboldt A Von: Ponts de partage et communications projetées between the Grand Océan et l'Océan Atlantique 1808, Sherwood III RM: The Cartography of Alexander Von Humboldt: Images of the ... https: //books.google.com.co/ books?
isbn = 0549556540
Thesis U of Texas 2008.

Geographic Institute, Agustín Codazzi (Bogotá) Atrato-Truandó Department of Chocó, 1964.

Geographic Institute, Agustín Codazzi (Bogotá) Atrato-Truandó [cartographic material]: Department of Chocó / 1964

Interoceanic Canal Studies - 1970. Annex V. Study of Engineering Feasibility. Volume I. Appendix 1. Description of Routes; Appendix 2. Conventional Excavation Technology; Appendix 3. Nuclear Excavation Technology; Appendix 4. Project Management, Organization and Funding.

Kennish, W: The Practicability and Importance of a ship canal to connect the Atlantic & Pacific Oceans. Nesby, New York, 1855 (Google Books).

Kelley F.M., Kennish W., (CE) Serrel, E.W. The Practicability and Importance of a Ship Canal to Connect the Atlantic and Pacific Oceans. With instructions from F.M Kelley esq. to William Kennish esq., civil engineer. Nesby New York 1855.

Kelley, Frederick M, Kennish, William (1855)
Interoceanic Canal of Colombia: Discovery and Exploration of the Interoceanic Canal Vía Atrato-Truandó. Editorial National University of Colombia. (Bogota, 2013 -
http://www.bdigital.unal.edu.co/12339/

Kelley Frederick - Wikipedia, the free encyclopedia https://en.wikipedia.org/wiki/ Frederick_Kelley, May 2015).
Laboratoire Central Hydraulique de France, Paris. Project of Chocó development. Study of the Atrato-San Juan waterway, channels, locks. Preliminary report. Bogota 1966.

Landazábal Reyes, F.L. The channel of the Atrato. Army Magazine, No. May 18, (1964).

Laverde Goubert, L. The Chocó Canal. Armed Forces Magazine, Vol. 10 No. Nov. 29-Dec, (1964).

Laverde Goubert, L. Ideas on the Chocó Canal. Rev Armed Forces, 1964; 9 (26): 383-392 (Thesis and academic dissertations). Thesis Note: Thesis (Lawyer) - Universidad La Gran Colombia.

Malte-Brun VA: Du Projet de Communication Interocéanique par l'Isthme de Darien. Bull Soc Géographique de Paris 1857.

Mariño Sánchez, J. Will the construction of the Atrato Canal be possible? / 1961.

Martínez Landinez J: COLOMBIAN GEOPOLITICS. Delivery No. 6. The Interoceanic Route of Colombia Called Atrato-Truandó from the Gulf of Urabá-Río ... 1959.

McCullough, D. The Path Between the Seas. Simon & Schuster, NY, 2001.

Mejía, LG: "The Interoceanic Canal". El Colombiano Octubre 4, 2011.

Mendoza Morales, A. El Canal: Atrato- Truandó / 1996.

Meyer Victoria: Research Assistant at JPL "Forest Structure and Biomass: GeoSAR Measurements in Chocó, Colombia" https://nisar.jpl.nasa.gov/nisarworkshop2015_posters.html

Michler, N: Report of Lieutenant Nathaniel Michler of a survey for an Interoceanic Ship Canal. December,1887.

Michler, N: Report of the secretary of war, communicating, in compliance with a resolution of the Senate, Lieutenant Michler's ... Michigan Historical Reprint Series, Michigan Publishing 2005.

Ministry of Public Works: Canal del Atrato: exposure to the bill that authorizes the National Governor to prepare studies of an Interoceanic Canal, through the Hoya del Río Atrato and through the Serranía del Baudó 1964 ...

Ministry of Public Works Colombia. Interoceanic sea-level channel studies. Technical reports summaries. Bogota, October,1978.

Ministry of Public Works. Study of the Atrato-Truandó Channel, Bogotá, Colombia, 1969.

Ministry of Public Works. Colombia Interoceanic sea-level channel studies. Technical reports summaries. Bogotá, October,1978.

United States. Atlantic-Pacific Interoceanic Canal Study Commission. Seven volumes, Washington, DC 1970.

Molano A, Ramírez MC: The Darién Gap, a journey diary. Biology Texts, César **Monje:** The Seal Ed. Bogotá 1996.

Molano Campuzano, J. Travel of Leonese Wafer to the Isthmus of Darien (Four months among the Indians). Bulletin 4 Year XI, 1953.

Monsalve Cuberos, L. The Atrato-Truandó Bol Sogeocol Interoceanic Canal, 1982; 36 (117).
Moreno, JA: Act of Constitution and Statutes Interoceanic Canal Atrato-Truandó, CANATCOL, AP. https: // issuu.com/jimgomez/docs/ acta_const_11.26.15

Mosquera JC of: President of New Granada, Honorary Member of the Society of Practical Agronomy of Paris: Memory on the Physical and Political Geography of New Granada. Dedicated to the Geographical and Statistical Society of New York, New York 1852.

Mosquera Rivas, R: Opportunity to build the Atrato-Truandó Canal, Bol Sogeol 1981; 35 (115).

Mosquera Rivas, R: Channel level in Colombia. Bol. Sogecol 1982; 36 (117).

Mosquera Rivas, R. Canal at the Colombian level: National Forum on Chocó Development / 1982.

Mosquera Rivas, R. The forum on the Interoceanic Canal Atrato-Truandó, Bol Sogecol 1984-1985; 37 (119-120).

Munera Mouthon, P.A. The forum on the Interoceanic Canal Atrato-Truandó, Bol Sogeocol 1984-1985; 37 (119-120).

Nourse JE: Interoceanic communication across Central America, Civil <mech Eng 1872; 62: 383.

Obregón Andreu, Mauricio, (1921-1998) Canal Atrato, Colombia. # Clasif. B 46361, 1964.

Ortega, Alfredo: The Interoceanic Canal by the Atrato, An Ing Bogotá 1930; 38 (451): 337-342.

Ortiz Restrepo, C. About the new Chocó Canal / 1966.

Ossa Varela, P. Report of the engineer Peregrino Ossa Varela to the Ministry of Industry / 1934.

Ossa V., Pilgrim: Interoceanic Canal by the Atrato, An Ing Bogotá 1941; 49 (562): 691-692.

Páez G: Commentary on Law 53 of 1984. Bol Sogecol 1985; 37 (119-120).

Palacios Martínez, D: El Canal Atrato- Truandó
ORDERED BY LAW 53 OF 1984, Bulletin of the Geographic Society of Colombia 1984-1985; 7 (119-120).
Panero, R.: Development project for the Chocó (some aspects on the construction of an interoceanic passage through the Deacó del Chocó, Colombia, New York, Hudson Institute 1966.

Peralta, J.A. The Interoceanic Canal: concrete giant or mega project of life? /1999.

Pitman, Robert Birks. A succinct view and analysis of authentic information extant in original works, on the practicability / of joining the Atlantic and Pacific Oceans, by ship canal across the isthmus of America London: printed for JM Richardson and J. Hatchard, 1825. viii, 229 p., 11. 1 map. 8th. TSB.

Puydi L: L'Isthme Américain et le channel Colombienne. Percement du Darien Châtillon sur Seine, Cornillac 1869.

Quijano O, J.M. Report on the exploration of the isthmus of Panama and Darién, in the Official Gazette of the United States of Colombia (Bogotá, 1875), p. 2785 et seq.

Quintero, J. Scientific artistic concept of the Atrato-Truandó Canal map. Bol Sogecol 1984-1985; 37 (119-120).

Ramírez, J.E. Atrato-Truandó Interoceanic Canal Project (Colombia) at sea-level. Bol. Sogecol, 1967, 25 (95-96).

Reclus E: Colombia, (T) Vergara and Velasco FJ. Pap, Tint, Bogota 1893 [Dedicated to the Colombian geographer Agostino Codazzi, in its first centenary] Google ebooks.

Restrepo Uribe, J. Canal Atrato-Truandó, Editor: Leanló, 1983.

Restrepo, R.L: Solano Bay and its possible interoceanic communications with the Atrato River. Sogecol Bowl 1938; 5 (1).

Rodrigue, JP: The Expanded Panama Canal. Initial Impacts on North American Ports. Policy Integration and Research, Transport Canada, 2019.

Samper Pizano E: SAMPER'S PROPOSAL TO LIVE THE PROJECT OF AN INTEROCEANIC CANAL FROM URABA TO THE PACIFIC RESULTS AS SOPRESSELY AS LITTLE VIABLE., Week 1996/06/24.

Sánchez Montenegro, V.: Background of the Panama Canal and the Atrato. Armed Forces Magazine, Vol. 9 No. 27 Jul.-Aug. (1964).

Sanclemente, C. The channel of the Atrato / 1983.

Santander, L.J. The Canal of the Atrato, colossal work. Forces Magazine Armed, Vol. 10 No. Sep. 28-Oct. (1964).

Schlubach, R. Carlos, W. Very important aspects of the Atrato canal. Sogeocol Bowl 1986; 38 (121).
Schlubach, R. Carlos, W.: The development of Urabá, Darién and Chocó Norte and its importance in helping to build the Atrato-Truandó Canal. Bol Sogecol 1986; 38: 121.
Serrano Avila, R: The Atrato Canal. Armed Forces Magazine, Vol. 42 No. 124, Jul.-Sep. (1987).

Silva Sánchez, G. Atrato-Truandó Canal Forum. Monetarism or Canal: Colombia must choose. Bol Sogecol 1986; 38 (121).

Silva, Betancourt: At Atrato-Truandó Interoceanic Canal, Development Pole 1989, Geographical Society of Colombia: Convenience and opportunity to study the possible Interoceanic Canal by the 1937 Atrato; Bowl 1; Four.

Society of Geography of Colombia: Prospective. Atrato-Truandó Interoceanic Canal, Bol Sogeocol 1986; 38 (121).

Society of Geography of Colombia Colombian Society of Engineers, Fusion Energy Foundation Public Declaration approved by the Forum on the Atrato Canal meeting in Bogotá on August 8 and 9, 1985, Bol Sogeocol 1984-1985; 37, (119).

Society of Geography of Colombia, Bulletin (Bogotá). - Vol. 6, No. 2-3 (Jun./Dec. 1939). - p. 2-3.

Society of Geography of Colombia Convenience and opportunity to study the possible Interoceanic Canal through the Atrato. Sogeocol Bowl 1934; 4: (1). Geographical Society of Colombia Ignorance about Colombia. La Hilea Magdalenense / El Canal del Atrato, Intercontinental and interoceanic communication routes Bol. Sogeocol 1948; 8: (1).

"Special Report of the Governor of the Panama Canal on the Atrato-Truandó Canal Route, Under Public Law 280.79th Congress, 1949"

https://www.govinfo.gov/content/pkg/GOVPUB- M115-
28ef053b58bcf87d5bcd496b093d67
88 / pdf / GOV PUB- M115-28ef053b58bcf87d5bcd496b093d67 88.pdf

Teller DW: Interoceanic Canal: project proposed to the National Congress of the United States of Colombia by Daniel W. Teller, of New York, a North American citizen, for the conclusion of a privilege contract for the excavation of an Interoceanic Canal. Echeverria Hnos Printing, Bogota 1866 www.banrepcultural.org/.../canal- interocean.

Torres Sánchez J, Salazar HLA: Introduction to the History of Engineering and Education in Colombia Univ Nal de Col, Bogotá 2002.

Trautwine JC: Rough notes of an exploration for an interoceanic canal route by way of the rivers Atrato and San Juan, in New Granada, South America 1882 United States. Department of State Isthmus of Darien - ship channel. Message from the President of the United States, transmitting the information required by a resolution of the House of representatives of the 17th last, in relation to a ship canal across the Isthmus of Darien. 25th Cong., 2d sess. House. Doc. 228https: //hdl.handle.net/2027/ uc1.b4915606? Urlappend =% 3Bseq = 213.

US Commission for Interoceanic Canal Studies, 1970
ufdc.ufl.edu/AA00006086/00001 Pacific Interoceanic Canal Study. Commission as required by Public Law 88-609 ...... area includes the homelands of Chocó and Cuna Indian tribes Blanco-Libreros JF et al.

U.S. Statutes at Large, 39th Congress, 2nd Session, volume 14, page 567 [Do not. 26.] Ship Canal across the Isthmus of Darien. A resolution to extend aid and facilities to citizens of the United States engaged in the survey of a route for a ship canal across the Isthmus of Darien. February 25, 1867. http://memory.loc.gov/cgi-bin/ampage? collId = llsl & fileName = 014 / llsl014.db & recNum = 598.

Valencia Tovar, A. The Interoceanic Canal, a national objective. Armed Forces Magazine, Vol. 9 No. May 26-Jun. (1964).

Valois Arce, D: Atrato Canal. Ed Kealon Medellin 1981.

Von Humboldt, Alexander, Political Essay on the Kingdom of New Spain, 1811.

Wafer, L: Voyage and description of the Isthmus of Darien, London 1699.

Wyse, Lucien Napoleón Bonaparte, and others. Interocéanique Channel 1877-1878. Rapports sur les études of the Commission internationale d'exploration de L'isthme américain. Paris: A. Lahure, 1879. 294 p., 1 1., 1 map, 1 pi. sq. 4th. f TSB.

14. ACKNOWLEDGEMENTS

Mrs. Lorena Gómez asked us why we had not written a book about the Interoceanic Canal. She illustrated us in the way books are currently made and encouraged us to carry out this work that we prepared with pleasure to celebrate the II Centenary of the Independence of Colombia. She has been kind enough to correct and put the manuscript in the proper way to publish it in the new methods.

We appreciate the help of many librarians who have provided us with references in Colombia and abroad. To the authors who have allowed us to publish illustrations. To Dr. Juan Felipe Blanco Libreros (juan.blanco@udea). With sincere thanks for his authorization to publish the illustrations of Bathymetry: Blanco Libreros JF, Londoño Mesa MH: "South Caribbean Expedition: Antioquia and Chocó coastal" -tesis.udea.edu.co, Medellín, Colombia 2016) and all our collaborators who have made this work possible. To the artist Luz H. Flórez for modifying the Shield of Colombia and to Mrs. Guiomar Flórez Mariño for the cover of the book. Last but not least, we thank Dr. Joaquín Catalá Alís, Professor of the Department of Construction Engineering and Civil Engineering Projects of the Polytechnic University of Valencia, Spain for kindly writing the foreword of the book.

The authors

AMGD